DISCOVERING WORDS

D1374967

Julian Walker

SHIRE PUBLICATIONS

First published in Great Britain in 2009 by Shire Publications Ltd, Midland House, West Way, Botley, Oxford OX2 0PH, United Kingdom.
443 Park Avenue South, New York, NY 10016, USA.

E-mail: shire@shirebooks.co.uk   www.shirebooks.co.uk

Every attempt has been made by the Publishers to secure the appropriate permissions for materials reproduced in this book. If there has been any oversight we will be happy to rectify the situation and a written submission should be made to the Publishers.

A CIP catalogue record for this book is available from the British Library.

Shire Discovering no. 300   •   ISBN-978 0 74780 749 0

Julian walker has asserted his right under the Copyright, Designs and Patents Act, 1988, to be identified as the author of this book.

Designed by Ken Vail Graphic Design, Cambridge, UK and typeset in Perpetua and Gill Sans.
Printed in Malta by Gutenberg Press Ltd.

09 10 11 12 13   10 9 8 7 6 5 4 3 2 1

ACKNOWLEDGEMENTS
With thanks to Peter Doyle, Anne Eggebert, John Frankis and staff at the British Library.

DEDICATION
For Liz and Peter F. Walker.

Contents

Introduction

WHEN we speak English we benefit from over twenty-five centuries of living culture, though we seldom think about where the words we use come from or how they got to us. But the study of the history of words reveals extraordinary and often unexpected voyages across time and space. The richness of the English language as seen in the extent of its vocabulary comes from a history of the movement of people across boundaries, the sharing of ideas and the vigour of enquiring minds. Writing and speaking English is the celebration of this history.

When we sit on the sofa to watch the television screen while eating a pizza or curry, hoping the phone will not ring, we are using words borrowed or constructed from a wide range of languages. Some of them we recognise as foreign in origin, because they somehow do not sound English, while others have become so naturalised through use that they appear to be quintessentially English. They may have come directly or via one or more other languages ('screen'), may have displaced other words ('sofa' for 'settle'), may have come as part of war, migration or colonisation ('curry'), or been consciously invented to supply the need for naming a technological invention ('phone'). They may even combine roots from two or more languages ('television'), or be in the process of change through which clear evidence of their origin may be lost ('when').

Sometimes the journeys of words are unexpected. 'Pizza' is derived ultimately from a language very similar to English (and is related to the word 'bite'), yet retains an unmistakably Italian feel. 'Eat' may sound a basic Germanic type of word, similar to the German *essen*, but can be traced back to similar words in Latin and Greek, and beyond to Sanskrit, one of the world's oldest languages, used in northern India since over three thousand years ago. A word may travel from the British Isles to a language in another country and come back to English many centuries later; this has happened for many of the words of Celtic origin in English, other than place-names.

There are many reasons for the richness of English. Waves of immigration and invasion brought the dialects spoken by various groups of people from the area covering present-day coastal Belgium, Holland, northern Germany and Denmark into contact with a mixture of Celtic and Latin, soon dominating or excluding them and creating what we know as Old English, or Anglo-Saxon (to avoid confusion, I shall use 'Old English' for the language, 'Anglo-Saxon' for the people); later invasions from Scandinavia and France changed the language both structurally and in terms of vocabulary. New words arrived later with the propensities for trade, colonisation, conquest, travel and invention, which have characterised British history.

Ideas as well as items bring new words, for how else can they be discussed and used? The seventeenth and eighteenth centuries brought extensive and innovative thinking in the fields of arts and architecture, science, philosophy, politics and engineering, all fields requiring an extensive new vocabulary. Often words were borrowed directly from other languages – 'calibre' and 'bayonet' from French, 'miniature' from Italian, 'veneer' from German. Or a word might emerge from academia to fit a new way of thinking, such as 'democracy'; a word newly invented in another language, such as 'oxygen', might travel across national boundaries, sometimes, as in the case of 'gin', deriving from the place of origin of the idea or invention. Or a new concept, such as 'microscope', might require the construction of a new word from words in another language, usually Latin or Greek, reflecting the esteem in which these languages were held.

From early on, the names of traded goods have been added to the English lexicon, while from the late Middle Ages words arrived that form a historical map of the growth of what would become the British Empire. Both of these chart the interaction between Britain and the rest of the world in terms other than migration. New practices from abroad tended to arrive with their own words. French clothes fashion brought 'petticoat', Italian garden design brought 'patio' and 'gazebo', while Dutch marine engineering brought 'pump' and 'derrick'. Foods and materials, such as 'tomato' or 'denim', might come with a name which would be anglicised beyond recognition, through spelling or pronunciation or both.

Advances in science, engineering and technology have always required the invention of new words or the borrowing of foreign ones, from the 'cannon' of the sixteenth century, borrowed from French, to the 'internet' of the twentieth century, reputedly coined by the United States Defense Department. The adoption of brand names for generic usage dates back to the rise of branded goods in the nineteenth century, including 'aspirin' in 1899, and 'linoleum' as early as 1864.

There is a well-known idea that the Norman Conquest brought about a two-tier linguistic structure reflecting the two-tier social structure; in this, the Norman lord of the manor ate 'beef', from an animal tended by his Saxon serf, who called it a 'cow'. But all levels of society had to 'cook', from Latin via Old English, and 'eat', which is related to both early Germanic and Latin. In a delightful twist, the later French nickname for an English person, *un rosbif*, comes from 'roast' and 'beef', both words which came to English from French.

Language has always been used to mark distinction and exclusivity, as well as to communicate. In the sixteenth and seventeenth centuries a great debate went on over the creation of new Latin-based words; some of them were accepted into common usage, while others remained for a short time the preserve of scholars, before disappearing altogether. In more recent times we have grown used to the idea of jargon being used to exclude or overwhelm the uninitiated, whether it be Cockney rhyming slang, the acronyms produced by government, or the terms used in the local hardware store.

There is a story that Queen Anne in 1710 described St Paul's Cathedral as 'terrible and awful'; the variations of vocabulary in different versions of the story indicate that it probably did not take place, but it still serves to illustrate a point about how the meanings of words change. In the early eighteenth century this description meant that the building inspired awe and wonder, much as we might say 'awesome and terrific'. These two pairs of words come from the same root, but have acquired completely opposite meanings, comparatively recently. It is a process that occurs frequently with slang – currently 'wicked' means something far from 'evil', while someone can be described with approval as simultaneously both 'cool' and 'hot'.

From one root a word can diverge into different, even contradictory, applications: 'person', coming from the Latin *persona*, a mask worn in the theatre by an actor, became at the same time the word for the character in a drama, and the living body of an individual. Shakespeare used both meanings, referring to 'our person' for the body of King Henry V, and Quince in *A Midsummer Night's Dream* presenting 'the person' of Moonshine.

'Discuss', coming from Latin words meaning 'to break apart', was used by Chaucer in the fourteenth century to mean 'to disperse' or 'dispel', from which it developed to 'to examine by argument, investigate or decide', close to the modern meaning of considering a matter calmly.

There are still those who feel that if English were 'fixed', the benefits in comprehension would outweigh the disadvantages. In 1651 John Cheke wrote: 'I am of this opinion that our own tung should be written cleane and pure, unmixt and unmangeled with borrowing of other tunges…' But according to Bill Bryson the language is currently adopting up to twenty thousand new words every year, as many as Shakespeare used in all his works. New words will influence the existing vocabulary, and the likelihood of a fixed set of spellings, meanings and usages is as remote now as it was when in 1712 Jonathan Swift complained about 'a succession of affected phrases, and new, conceited words'.

How English has changed

It is possible that the Celtic-speaking Britons, not being the first inhabitants of Britain, took over existing place-names, but these are no longer distinguishable. The words from pre-Roman cultures that have survived are mostly place-names or to do with the natural environment. Celtic words that have survived include 'crag', 'brock' (badger) and 'coomb', but many words came later from Celtic to English via other languages – 'embassy' via French and Latin, 'cargo' via Spanish, and 'caricature' via Italian. The 350 years of Roman rule in Britain would have affected Celtic, as it affected the Germanic languages of northern Europe, and a few remnants of these remain, particularly in place-names.

It is from about fifteen hundred years ago that we can date a language identifiable, though not yet recognisable, as English. The Germanic settlers of the time brought with them a variety of dialects, about which little is known, but from these emerged the language we know as Old English, whose first written texts date from the seventh century. Many of these migrants brought with them Latin words which they had acquired through trade and contact, words such as 'mill' and 'pound'. The extent and success of the Germanic social and linguistic takeover can be seen in the word 'Welsh', describing one group of the earlier inhabitants who had been driven to the edge of the island: the word is Old English for 'foreign'.

The spread of Christianity from the sixth century brought some liturgical Latin to Old English, but for legal and administrative purposes most new words were formed from existing Old English roots. From the middle of the ninth century Scandinavian or Norse invaders and settlers came to the north and east of England bringing a language that had evolved from the same roots as Old English. The mix of the two gave rise to some hybridisation, while the enlargement of the lexicon from population intermingling gave the possibility of two words for essentially the same thing, with the potential for distinction of meaning, as in 'skin' (from the Norse) and 'hide' (from Old English). Sometimes a word was adopted in two forms, giving divergent meanings, such as 'skirt' and 'shirt'.

The arrival of a French-speaking governing class in 1066 marks the beginning of the gradual change to what we know as Middle English; from this period Old English was replaced by Latin as the language of administration, while Anglo-Norman took over as the spoken language of the ruling class, and the language of literature and, later on, the administration of manors and taxes; as the languages merged through social interaction, a doubling of the lexicon occurred again. The extensive grammatical system of changing word-endings in Old English died out, as word order became fundamental in structuring the meaning of sentences.

For about 150 years the status of English, the language spoken by the vast majority of the people, is unclear, so little writing having survived. As Anglo-Norman declined, so Middle English developed, until around the end of the fourteenth century it began to be used for administration. However, during this period, thousands of words came from French into English; many of these had originated in languages spoken in distant areas many centuries earlier, such as Arabic, Greek or Sanskrit.

From the thirteenth to the early seventeenth century the sound of the vowels in spoken English changed. Though political and other upheavals such as the Black Death brought about changes and migrations in the workforce in England and elsewhere, no simple reason can be given for the Great Vowel Shift. Long vowels came to be vocalised higher in the mouth and changed into diphthongs (double vowel sounds); for example Middle English *fif*, rhyming with 'leaf' and 'chief' in modern Received Pronunciation, changed to late sixteenth-century 'five', rhyming with modern RP 'hive' and 'alive'.

The advent of printing in the fifteenth and sixteenth centuries brought about some standardisation in the language, and the dominance of the dialect of the London area. The spread of classical learning and the increasing cultural influence of Italy led to the 'inkhorn terms' debate over the desirability or otherwise of so many new Latin-based terms, a debate which was repeated in the nineteenth century by campaigners for a supposedly purer non-Latin lexicon. The brilliant rise of literature in English from *Piers Plowman* in the middle of the fourteenth century, including Chaucer, Wycliffe and Tyndale, the translators of the Bible, to Spenser, Marlowe and Shakespeare brought about an explosion of new vocabulary in English. Shakespeare alone is believed to have introduced over fifteen hundred new words. There were moves towards the end of the sixteenth century to regularise English spelling, by Mulcaster and others, as part of the move towards raising the status of English in schools; but the vagaries of compositors meant that printing did less to support this than might be expected.

The Enlightenment, the Industrial Revolution and the growth of the British Empire led to two different kinds of growth in the language. New fields of science, technology and intellectual investigation required new words; and contact with people in all parts of the world brought vocabulary for goods, processes and activities that often arrived through other languages. Thus the word 'sequin' arrived from Arabic via Italian and French.

The eighteenth and nineteenth centuries brought two great debates about how the English language should progress. Firstly, should there be a 'fixing' of the language, a defining of what was 'good' English? Samuel Johnson's *Dictionary of the English Language,* first published in 1755, set a standard for the spelling and meaning of English words, provoking reactions from many writers, including Noah Webster, the editor of the famous 1828 *American Dictionary of the English Language.* The second debate was similar to the 'inkhorn' debate of earlier times, a move to reject the increasing flow of Latinate words in favour of Old English word construction, on the basis of an idea that these were more 'natural' to English. As late as 1906, Fowler's *The King's English* was advising people to 'prefer the Saxon word to the Romance'.

The vast increase in the number of people speaking English has led to borrowings from indigenous languages, this especially being the case in colonised areas of Africa, Asia and America where societies were already multilingual, and where borrowings and influences between languages were common. In some cases words entered English which had been created within a pidgin (a language created from other languages which has no native speakers), of which English was one of the constituents.

Where people have moved away from the United Kingdom and established populations centred elsewhere, the changes in the language at home have not been repeated in new settlements. Thus American English retains a number of words that were common in British English hundreds of years ago but have been superseded; 'trash' and 'fall' were both common in English in the seventeenth century but have now been replaced in Britain by 'rubbish' and 'autumn'. However, words that have been acquired by non-British English, for example 'stampede' and 'cafeteria', Spanish words in American English, have been later passed on to British English.

The movement of words globally continues as English becomes the dominant language of such worldwide fields as sport (Croatian *tenis*, French *le football*), the internet (Turkish *Internet)* and finance (German *die Finanz*). As more and more people around the world speak English as a second or third language, and as we invent new ways of communicating through language, such as computer chatrooms or text messaging, new words keep on being fed into the language from outside, or constructed from within, and English goes on growing.

A note on neighbouring languages and their periods

The changes in languages are slow, though they often result from a discrete political change, and the dates given are no more than convenient points during a period of change.

The Germanic group of languages, to which English belongs, is a branch of the Indo-European language family.

The Latin spoken in the Roman Empire differed varyingly from written Latin, known as Classical Latin; I have used the word Latin to refer to Classical Latin, and Greek for the Greek used in the last five hundred years BC.

The peoples who migrated from the Continent to England from around AD 450 spoke West Germanic dialects. It is now thought unlikely that they all spoke the same form of language, though nothing much is known about them before about 600. Their migration over a period of several hundred years was initially from the Danish peninsula and the coastal areas to the south-west as far as the mouth of the Rhine. Old English developed in different dialects throughout England, though early written texts are surprisingly similar, deriving mostly from the West Saxon area; but after the loss of status of English following the Norman Conquest it was the dialect of the East Midlands and London that became the antecedent of standard English.

Two geographically close languages that developed while Old English was developing in England were: *Old Frisian*, from about 700 to 1500, spoken along the coastline between the Rhine and the Elbe; *Old Saxon*, spoken up to about 1000 in the North Sea and other coastal areas of northern Germany.

Languages nearby that developed while Middle English was developing in England include: *Middle Low German*, spoken in the northern Germanic area (based around the North Sea and Baltic Sea) from about 1100 to 1600; *Middle Dutch*, used to the west, and *Middle High German*, to the south, from about 1100 to 1600. *Old Norse* was spoken in the Scandinavian countries from about 800 to 1300.

The westward migration of the Franks from Germany from the third century influenced the Latin spoken in northern France that they adopted, classed as *Late Latin*. This developed divergent forms in speech (*Vulgar Latin*) and writing (*Medieval Latin*); Vulgar Latin evolved into *Old French* around the ninth century. Medieval Latin continued to be used in Europe through the medieval period. *Norman French* was French spoken in Normandy as opposed to Parisian French; it was influenced by the Vikings who settled in Normandy. This was the language spoken by the Normans in England from 1066, but it developed mixed forms in Anglo-Norman. *Anglo-Norman* (sometimes called *Anglo-French*) was French spoken in England after 1066 and was influenced over time by Parisian French. *Parisian French* was spoken in northern France outside Normandy and Brittany during the medieval period. *Middle French* is considered to have lasted from about 1300 to 1600.

Gothic was the Germanic spoken by a group of peoples from eastern Europe, some of whom in the fifth century AD migrated west from the area of the Balkans to Italy, Spain and Portugal.

Acknowledgements

I have made frequent references in this book to dictionaries published between 1600 and the present. Chiefly they are by Robert Cawdrey (*A Table Alphabeticall of Hard Usual English Words*, 1604), John Bullokar (*The English Expositor*, 1616), H. Cockeram (*The English Dictionarie*, editions of 1623 and 1670), Stephen Skinner (*Etymologicon Linguae Anglicanae*, 1671), Nathaniel Bailey (*An Universal Etymological English Dictionary*, 1721), Samuel Johnson (*A Dictionary of the English Language*, 1755, plus editions of 1773, 1790, and Fulton's miniature edition of 1822), Noah Webster (*A Compendious Dictionary of the English Language*, 1806; *An American Dictionary of the English Language*, first edition 1828, tenth edition 1832), Andrew Findlater (*Chambers Etymological Dictionary of the English Language*, 1882), H. W. Fowler and F. G. Fowler (*The Concise Oxford Dictionary of Current English*, 1974), and the *Oxford English Dictionary* in editions from 1971 and 1989 and online, particularly for its documentations of dated usage.

Etymology has been the subject of countless works of scholarship; I have particularly referred to those by Isidore of Seville (*The Etymologies*, seventh century), Walter Skeat (*A Concise Etymological Dictionary of the English Language*, 1882), Hensleigh Wedgwood (*Contested Etymologies*, 1882), Abram Palmer (*Folk-etymology*, 1882), Otto Jesperson (*The Growth and Structure of the English Language*, 1912), Mary Serjeantson (*A History of Foreign Words in English*, 1935), C. T. Onions (*The Oxford Dictionary of English Etymology*, 1966), J. A. Sheard (*The Words We Use*, 1970), Eric Partridge (*Origins*, 1982), Adrian Room (*Dictionary of True Etymologies*,

1986), and Alexander Tulloch (*Word Routes*, 2005). I have also referred to histories of the English language, including *A History of the English Language* (1993) by Albert Baugh and Thomas Cable, *Mother Tongue* (1990) by Bill Bryson, *The Cambridge History of the English Language* (2001), *The Cambridge Encyclopaedia of the English Language* (2002), *The Stories of English* (2004) by David Crystal, and *The Adventure of English* (2004) by Melvyn Bragg.

Pronunciation and spelling

In varying degrees, the Roman alphabet does not contain characters or combinations that correspond exactly to the sounds or signs of Old English or Old Norse, or to those of Greek, Arabic, Hebrew or Sanskrit. I have followed the usual simplifications and transcriptions into the modern Roman alphabet.

In Old and Middle English the letter *e* after a final consonant was pronounced as in the modern word 'the'. The Old English letter *æ*, which I have retained, was pronounced as a short vowel; the letter *þ* (voiced *th*) I have written as *th*; and ð (unvoiced *th*) I have written as *th*.

Arts and
Communication

Bulletin. The Latin word *bulla*, meaning 'bubble', possibly originally in imitation of the sound, has been the root for several English words. In Medieval Latin it came to mean 'seal' and as such entered Middle English as *bulle*. In Latin this meaning extended into the entire document to which the seal was attached, as in the Papal Bull which nullified Magna Carta. A small document became the Italian *bulleta*, which provided a further diminutive, *bulletino*, which came through French to English in the seventeenth century, when it was often spelt 'bolletine'; by the early eighteenth century the spelling was established as 'bulletin'.

Cinema. The abbreviated form of 'cinematograph', this word is an anglicisation of the French *cinématographe*, the word used by the brothers Lumière to describe their invention in 1896. The Greek word *kinema* means 'movement', giving the adjective *kinemato-*, to which is added *graph*, meaning 'drawing'. The abbreviation 'cinema' was not used until 1910, but in some cases the spelling 'kinema' was preferred, perhaps in an attempt to give respectability to a popular medium by referencing the Greek origins of the word. The *Merriam-Webster Online Dictionary* gives 'kinema' as a British variant spelling, and anyone looking up 'cinema' in the 1979 compact version of the *OED* will be referred to 'kinema'.

Critic. Webster linked 'critic' to 'crime', but the connection to 'crisis' made in his entry for 'critical' would have been closer. The Greek word *krisis* means a 'sifting', thus figuratively an 'act of discrimination', appropriately carried out by a 'critic'. The date of its adoption into English, at the end of the sixteenth century, would seem to indicate that this was one of the inkhorn terms loved by some scholars and hated by others, and thus itself subject to the opinions of 'critics'. A number of forms were used: *criticus* from Latin, *critique* from French, as well as 'critic' and 'critick'. Johnson tried to fix the spelling with the by then fairly out-of-date form 'critick', but it did not stick.

Dialogue. The supposition that the *di* in dialogue means 'two' is misleading; the Greek root *dia* meaning 'through' or 'between' provides a component of many more English words than *di*. Thus, a 'dialogue', properly speaking, may be between any number of people. However, probably by association with *di* as 'two', early on in its use in English the idea took hold of a 'dialogue' being a conversation between specifically two people. 'Dialogue' comes from the Greek *dialogos* through Latin *dialogum* to French *dialogue*. It first appeared in English in the fifteenth century. The *dia-* prefix, meaning 'through', also appears in 'diagram', 'dialect', 'diaphragm' and 'diarrhoea'.

Easel. In art-school life classes an 'easel' can be either something the student stands at or a bench to sit astride, with the drawing-board propped in front, in which case it is called a 'donkey'. The Latin *asinus* became the Old English *assa* and the Middle English *asse*, meaning 'ass or donkey'; the diminutive form *asellus* became in Dutch *ezel*, 'little donkey', and specifically the artist's 'easel'. In the seventeenth and eighteenth centuries the spelling varied, including 'easel', 'easle' and 'ezel'. The spelling may have adapted to include the sense of 'ease' that the apparatus brought to the artist's task. A number of combination words also use the word 'horse' to describe something acting as a frame or support.

Edit. In the early eighteenth century there were 'editors' before the word 'edit' had been coined. The root words had been around for much longer: the Latin *edere*, 'to publish', from words meaning 'out' and 'give', became the Old French *edicion* or *edition*. It was a fairly late arrival in English, first being recorded as 'edition' in 1551 in the sense of 'publishing'. The verb 'to edit' meaning 'to publish' is documented from 1791, and the specific sense of 'to prepare for publication' appeared in 1793. The use of 'to edit' meaning 'deliberately to alter how a text is received' appeared towards the end of the nineteenth century, though Webster in 1828 recognised that editing might involve a process of selection.

Jukebox. The 'box' in 'jukebox' is a music-making machine that replaced live musicians in a cheap roadside club providing live music, food and drinks, originally for African Americans in the early twentieth century. The word 'juke' was previously 'joog', a Gullah word derived from the word *dzug*, meaning 'to live wickedly', from the Wolof language of West Africa. During the period of enslavement it was the custom, when transporting captive people from Africa, to split up groups of people with a common language, to prevent onboard uprisings; the result was a pidgin (a lingua franca using simple words and little grammar, spoken as a second language) which became the Creole (subsequent first language of a community) known as Gullah, which is still spoken around the coastal area of South Carolina and Georgia, the area where most of the slave ships arrived in America.

Margin. In the eighteenth century 'margin' began to take the place of the more common 'margent', this change being reflected in the dictionaries of the time; Cawdrey (1604), Bullokar (1616) and Skinner (1671) all give 'margent', while Bailey (1721) gives 'margent or margin', and Johnson (1755) offers 'marge, margent and margin'. Webster (1828) gives only 'margin', but 'marge' is still included in Cooley's 1861 *Chambers Dictionary*. Around the same time the meaning broadened to include the sense of 'the state of danger of becoming excluded from the main body'. The word developed from Anglo-Norman forms *margin*, *margine* and *margene*, ultimately deriving from the Latin *margo*, meaning 'edge'.

Miniature. Despite immediate impressions, 'miniature' has no etymological link with 'mini'. It comes from a Medieval Latin term describing working on illuminated manuscripts in red, using 'minium', or red pigment. This pigment was originally cinnabar (mercuric oxide), but later the word was used for the much cheaper lead oxide. Cinnabar was one of the most brilliant and expensive pigments used on decorated manuscripts and was thus used sparingly, in such small quantities that the word 'minium' became the root for 'working small' in any medium. The sixteenth- and seventeenth-century forms 'miniture' and 'minuture' were temporary attempts to make sense of the spelling after the arrival of imports of cochineal from America had made obsolete the link between brilliant red and restrictive expense.

Nickname. This is one of a handful of examples of words which used to begin with a vowel, but where the *n* of the indefinite article has moved across and attached itself to the beginning of the word. 'A nickname' was 'an eke-name', and one of the first documentations of the word, in 1440, makes this clear: 'Neke name, or eke name' (*OED*). 'A vile ekename', as it appeared in 1303, was literally 'an extra name', *eke* meaning 'also'; it is related to the German for 'also', *auch*. It is found in Old English as *eac*, but occurs in *Beowulf* also as *ac*.

Pencil. Originally a paintbrush, from the Latin *penicillus*, meaning 'little tail', the word gradually came to be transferred to the hard graphite stick with a cover as this implement became more common. The word is related to 'penicillin', from the hair-like structure of the mould. The word entered Middle English from French as *pincel* in the early fifteenth century, becoming 'pencel' and then 'pensill' over the following two centuries. The first documented application of the word to a graphite stick in English was in 1612, but 'pencil' continued to be used for a small brush until the early nineteenth century. The original Latin root is possibly *penis,* meaning 'tail', with its diminutive *peniculus*, meaning 'brush'.

Piano. The *gravecembalo col piano e forte*, or 'harpsichord with soft and loud (pedals)', is noted in the *OED* from 1711, the key difference from previous keyboards being the possibility of controlling gradations of softness and loudness. This phrase was shortened in 1766 to *piano et forte*, which became the Italian and French *pianoforte* by 1771. At the same time the word *fortepiano* developed for the same instrument. The use of the word 'fortepiano' is confused and confusing: 'fortepiano' was formerly used from the point when the word had  dropped out of use (around the 1830s) to describe the earlier pianos used by composers from Haydn to Schubert, though the word 'pianoforte' was in use from when Haydn was a child. The *OED* records 'piano' in use from 1772.

Rhythm. In the Prologue to Ben Jonson's *Volpone* (1606) 'rhyme' is spelt 'ri'me', the apostrophe indicating a missing *th* sound. However, Mulcaster in 1582 spelled it 'rime', and Poole's *The English Parnassus* of 1677 has the word 'rhythm' in a position where it rhymes with 'crime'. In the seventeenth century the two words 'rhyme' and 'rhythm' had the same vowel sound and were only just beginning to diverge in terms of meaning; by the 1660s both words were used as a synonym for 'poetry'. They derive from the Latin *rhythmos*, originally a Greek word meaning 'rhythm' or 'symmetry', and appeared in English in the mid-sixteenth century.

Sketch. The Italian *schizzo* means 'sketch', but also a 'daub' or 'splash of mud', and the idea of a quick use of something liquid was for Wedgwood a fair reason to read this as the root of the word 'sketch'. For others it goes back to the Greek *skhedios*, which meant both 'near' and 'sudden', and which gave rise to *schizzo* and the Old French *esquiche*. The Dutch word *schets* could have influenced the form of the English word as it appeared in English in the early part of the seventeenth century when visual art contact between England and the Netherlands was strong; this would explain the early spelt forms 'scetch' and 'schetch'.

Talk. The Middle English *talkien* or *talken* derived, according to the *OED*, from the Old English *talian* and *tellan*, meaning 'to count, tell, calculate, think, argue', which is related to similar words meaning 'to speak, count or reckon' in other Germanic languages, especially Old Norse, where *tala* meant 'to relate or speak'. But other etymologists propose other derivations: for Tulloch it comes from the Lithuanian *tulkas*, meaning 'to talk', and is related to the Russian *tolk*, meaning 'sense'; while for Wedgwood the idea that so basic an activity should require a word from Lithuania is untenable. A link between Old English and the East Frisian word *talken*, meaning 'to talk', seems likely, but the word 'talk' in English is not recorded before the thirteenth century. However, it now falls within the five hundred most frequently used words in written English.

Television. Though the transmission of images by radio waves was not managed successfully until 1926, words to describe this had been around for much longer: as long as people had been struggling to bring the idea to realisation, so they strove to find a word for it. Constantin Perskyi is said to have used the word 'television' at the Paris World Fair in 1900, but previously Paul Nipkow had

experimented with what he called the 'electric telescope' in 1884, Sheldon Bidwell in 1881 had experimented with what he called 'telephotography', others had experimented with a 'telectroscope', and in 1862 Giovanni Caselli had transmitted a still image by what he called 'pantelegraph'. Other proposed names were 'tele-vista', 'radiovisor' and 'photo-telegraph'. The root that is common to almost all of the proposed terms, is *tele-*, the Greek for 'distant', connected eventually to 'vision', from the Latin for 'sight'. The combination of a Greek prefix and a Latin word has upset some people; T. S. Eliot described it as an example of a word that is 'ugly through foreignness or ill-breeding'.

Body and Health

Ache. Until the late sixteenth century 'ache' as a noun was pronounced as it was spelt, with a *tch* sound at the end; as a verb it was pronounced as now but was spelt 'ake' as late as the eighteenth century. This sound pattern for noun and verb is the same as can be seen in 'speech' and 'speak', but in the case of 'ache' spelling and spoken word became muddled around 1700. Effectively the spoken word 'ache' became obsolete, being replaced by the word 'ake'; and the spelling 'ake' became obsolete, being replaced by the spelling 'ache'. Johnson, trying to rationalise the etymology in his *Dictionary*, thought mistakenly that the word came from the Greek *achos*, meaning 'pain or distress', and declared both noun and verb 'more grammatically written "ache"'; but he still included an entry for the spelling 'ake'.

Bald. The proposal that the word 'bald' comes from the idea of a smooth round protuberance – a 'ball' – has some support; the earliest spelling, 'balled', gives the idea of something made 'like a ball', and this spelling was retained beyond Middle English, even being used as late as the end of the seventeenth century. But the *OED* points out the late appearance of the word 'ball', around 1300, which makes this difficult to sustain. The appearance of words beginning *bla-* to do with 'baldness' and 'white patches' in a number of nearby Germanic languages is used to support the idea that 'bald' comes from the idea of a 'white patch', surviving in the phrases 'bald-faced stag' and 'bald as a coot'. Partridge links the word to the Danish *baeldet*, meaning 'bald', and a possible Indo-European root *bhel-*, meaning 'to gleam'.

Blush. The Middle English *bluschen* meant 'to shine or become red', a development from the Old English *blyscan*, itself from *blysca* meaning 'flame'. It is linked to words in several Germanic languages to do with 'fire' and 'glowing red', such as the Old Norse *blys*, meaning 'torch', and Partridge notes a link to the word 'blaze'. For Johnson, one of its meanings was 'to carry a red colour' (tenth edition, 1790), but this presumably meant 'showing red'. Ben Jonson in 1625 coined the word 'blushet' for 'blushing girl', while the first documented use of cosmetic 'blusher' was in *Vogue* in 1965 (*OED*).

Cough. The Middle English *coughen* or *coghen* developed from the Old English *cohhetan*, meaning 'to cough or shout', and is related to Middle Dutch and Middle Low German *kuchen*, meaning 'to cough'. The noun 'cough' appeared in the fourteenth century. Most authorities agree that in all these languages the sound of the word imitates the sound of the action, the simplest spelling, 'cof', being recommended by Mulcaster in 1582. The Latin word for 'cough', *tussis*, which developed into Spanish *toser* and *tos* and French *tousser* and *toux* for 'to cough' and 'a cough' respectively, may also be imitative, but of a different, southern European kind of cough.

Face. This was the only part of the body for which a Norman introduction replaced an adequate choice of Old English words. The Saxons used the words *ansien, onsene, onsyn* and *wlite*, which disappeared, replaced by 'face' in its current spelling, documented from 1290 (*OED*). The ultimate root is the Latin *facies*, meaning 'form or shape', particularly the front of the head, deriving either from the verb *facere*, meaning 'to make', or from the root *fa-* meaning 'to shine'.

Gargle. With many words to do with the throat there is a clear sense of imitating the sound of the throat in action: *gargil*, a sixteenth-century word for 'gullet', from the Old French *gargouille* (translated alarmingly by Cotgrave as 'the weesle, or weason of the throat'[*OED*]); 'gargoyle', a waterspout shaped like a throat and mouth; 'gurgle', etc. 'Gargarise' or 'gargarize' was a word used by writers on health between about 1530 and 1720 to describe the act of 'wash[ing] or scour[ing] the mouth' (Bullokar, 1616). It was supplanted by 'gargle' perhaps because this form, described by the *OED* as 'more native', was more widely used in speech.

Inoculate. The process of 'inoculation' was brought to Britain in 1721 by Lady Mary Wortley Montague, the wife of the British ambassador to Turkey; she observed the practice in Turkey, where it had spread from India and China. The risky process involved injecting into a healthy person pathogens of a potentially fatal disease in the discharge of someone suffering from a mild case. The first documented use of this sense of 'inoculate' in English was in a *London Gazette* report on experiments applying the process to criminals in 1722, though the word 'inoculation' had been used in 1714. 'Inoculate' comes from the Latin *inoculare*, meaning 'to graft', used in the horticultural process of grafting a shoot of one plant (a scion) on to the stock of another (see **stock**); the Latin *oculus* meant 'bud' as well as 'eye'. This use of the word appeared in English in the fifteenth century.

Intestine. 'Intestine Broils allarm the Hive', wrote Dryden in 1697 (*OED*), meaning 'disturbances inside upset and provoke the beehive'; 'intestine' here was used figuratively to mean 'that which lies within', but by the mid-seventeenth century the word was being used to specify the 'alimentary canal'. The process of greater specification continued till by the mid-nineteenth century the 'intestines' were divided into 'the small and the large intestine', though some dictionaries were still using the singular form where we would use the plural. Johnson was perhaps ahead of his time in stating that the word was 'most commonly without a singular'. The word comes from the Latin *intestinus*, meaning 'internal'.

Lozenge. Johnson's *Dictionary* in 1822 defines 'lozenge' as a 'medicine made in small pieces to melt gradually in the mouth'. This is the fourth of Webster's five chronologically ordered definitions in the 1828 *Dictionary*, the first of which referred to the shape, deriving from Greek words for 'oblique' and 'corner'. Ivor Brown supports the idea that the word first meant a 'tombstone', for which a 'kite-shaped rhombus' might fit; certainly words based on *losa* or *lausa* in languages stretching from Portuguese to Provençal mean a 'slab' or 'tombstone'. A curious link with death is the fact that from the sixteenth century till the nineteenth widows' coats of arms were customarily framed within the shape of a lozenge. The word entered English from the French *losange*, becoming *losinge* in the fifteenth century, and was applied to a medicinal sweet in the sixteenth century – these being originally lozenge-shaped.

Moustache. The Middle French word *moustache* came directly into English and is recorded from about the end of the sixteenth century,

though the Old English had the words *granu* and *cenep*, from the Old Norse *knapr*. 'Moustache' came from the Italian *mostaccio*, itself from the Medieval Latin *mustacia*. These derive ultimately from the Greek *mustax*, meaning 'upper lip'. Variant spellings in the seventeenth century include 'mustages'.

Earlier British dictionaries and most American dictionaries preferred the spelling 'mustache' ('mustaches' in Johnson), and in American English the pronunciation is generally with a short *u*. Webster gives the word as plural only, which was in intermittent usage until recently (see **sideburns**).

Nightmare. One meaning for the Old English word *mara*, 'weight', brings the idea of something crushing a distressed sleeper, and Alexander Tulloch relates this idea to other European languages' words for 'nightmare' (*pesadilla* in Spanish, from *pesar*, meaning 'to weigh'), while the *mara* element is maintained in French *cauchemar* and Russian *koshmar*. Wedgwood points out that 'mare' also means 'ghost or hag' in several European languages, and that the nightmarish element of *cauchemar*, literally 'treading hag', is the second part. The *OED* definition of 'mare' in this sense is of a 'suffocating spirit experienced during sleep'. From the sixteenth century this was described as 'the nightmare' rather than 'a nightmare', as if it were an independent entity visiting itself upon sufferers.

Webster felt the spelling should be 'nightmar', though not from something that would 'mar' your night; he specified the experience of weight but put it down to 'usually the effect of indigestion or of a loaded stomach'.

Sideburns. Ambrose Burnside, a Union general during the American Civil War, had a magnificent set of whiskers growing at the side of his face (incidentally connected by a relatively discreet moustache). While he is commemorated by the word 'sideburns', perhaps the inversion of the word happened as a result of his disastrous defeat at the Battle of Fredericksburg in December 1862. A more likely explanation for the reconfiguration is by analogy to words such as 'sideshow', 'sidewalk' and 'side-pocket'.

Skeleton. The Greek word *skeletos*, from *skellein*, meaning 'to dry', gave rise to the Late Latin word *sceleton*, which was first used in English in the sixteenth century. The word was sometimes spelt *sc-* until the middle of the eighteenth century, though use of the *sk-* spelling dates from 1611; the first two vowels were rather more variable: 'sceleton', 'scelleton', 'scaleton', 'skelton', 'skeliton' and 'skelliton' all appear between 1578 and 1768. In the seventeenth and eighteenth centuries the form 'skelet' was used, but this survived only as a dialect form into the twentieth century.

Tablet. In 1843 William Brockenden took out an English patent for a machine that would 'shap[e] pills … by pressure in dies'; however, the tenth edition of Webster's *Dictionary* had included the definition for tablet as a 'medicine in square form' in 1832, and the *OED* gives the definition of 'medicine in the form of a small disc or lozenge' dating to 1564. These were presumably dried pastes or residues, rather than the compressed tablets which became widely available in the mid-nineteenth century. 'Tablet', which Webster also lists as meaning a 'small table or flat surface', and a 'surface for engraving, drawing or writing', comes from a diminutive form of the Latin *tabula*, meaning 'flat board'.

Tongue. There are no entries for 'tongue' in Webster's *Dictionaries*; instead the entries are for 'tung', with the note that 'our common orthography is incorrect; the true spelling is tung'. Webster resolutely maintained this spelling, as recommended by Mulcaster over two hundred years earlier, through several compound words, but it was not taken up, despite the *OED*'s declaration that 'tung' would be the 'natural' development of the spelling from Old English. The *OED* explains what happened: in Middle English and early Modern English the spelling changed from *tunge* to *tonge* and, to prevent a spelling that would give a final sound similar to that in 'lounge', something had to go between the *g* and the *e*. This gave rise to the spellings 'tounghe' and 'toungue', though it would have been easier simply to leave off the final *e*. Thus the spelling is 'neither etymological nor phonetic, and … only in a small degree historical' (*OED*).

Vaccinate. The legendary fair complexion of milkmaids was probably a result of their early unwitting 'vaccination' through handling contaminated milk with minor cuts on their hands, thus infecting themselves with cowpox and inoculating themselves against smallpox and avoiding its symptomatic pitting to the face (see **inoculate**).

Edward Jenner (1749–1823) used this information when in 1796 he took pus from the hand of Sarah Nelmes, a milkmaid suffering from cowpox, and inserted it into the arm of eight-year-old James Phipps, and effectively protected him against smallpox. 'Vaccinate' comes from the Latin *vacca*, meaning 'cow'. The word was used in a report on the process in 1800, but Jenner may have first used the word in his notes, though the treatment had been carried out by others previously.

Clothes and Fabrics

Apron. The Old French *naperon*, which was a diminutive form of the word *nape* or *nappe*, meaning 'tablecloth', became the Middle English *naperonn*. This was not so much a Norman import but a fashionable item borrowed from French custom. During the fifteenth century the *n* of *napron* started its transference across to the preceding article, against the pattern of 'nickname', where the *n* travelled in the other direction. The last recorded use of the word beginning with *n* is in 1569 (*OED*), by which time the variant spellings 'aprone', 'aperen', 'aparne' and 'appurn' were in use, as well as the spelling used now. Skinner and Johnson both proposed that the word derived from a contraction of the phrase 'afore-one'. (See **accomplice**, **umpire**.)

Button. Old French and Middle French *boton*, meaning 'bud', became the Middle English word *bouton*, a clothing innovation imported from France and restricted to the rich of medieval England, possibly originally as a decorative rather than a fastening device. It appeared in the fourteenth century and for a while retained also the meaning of 'flower-bud'. As a mechanical device, a 'button' is still essentially something that sticks out. The word appears in several languages in western Europe and derives from the Latin word *buttare*, meaning 'to thrust outwards', though ultimately the root word may have come from a Germanic source.

Collar. From the Latin word *collum*, meaning 'neck', developed the Old French and Middle French *colier* and *coler*, which became the Middle English *coler* and *coller*. The established spelling appeared in the early seventeenth century, but until that time the word was also applied to armour protecting the neck. The slang 'dog-collar' used in clerical dress was taken from the expression for existing fashionable close-fitting collars worn by both sexes in the late nineteenth century.

Corduroy. A real puzzle, 'corduroy' immediately looks like an anglicisation of the French for 'cord of the king'. Unfortunately no such fabric was invented in France, and the first mention of it in a list of fabrics made in France, in 1807, describes it as *kings-cordes*, indicating an English origin. There is a story that the fabric was designed by a Mr Corderoy, but no documentation to substantiate this survives. In the United States the name was given to a 'road made of logs', in imitation of the ribbed surface of the fabric.

Costume. 'Custom' and 'costume' are linked, and the etymology is easy to confuse. In Johnson's *Dictionary* in 1755 there is no entry for 'costume', nor a sense of a kind of dress in the entry for 'custom'. 'Costume' is recorded from 1715 as coming from both French and Italian, but in the sense of style pertaining to the dress, furniture or drapery of a particular historical period, and was applied to painting – a good historical painter would take care to show the right 'costume'. The first development from this was to different ways of dressing the hair, and from there to styles of clothing. But the first documented use for the dress particular to a nation, occupation or historical period was in 1802. The word is a development of the Italian *costume*, meaning 'custom, fashion or habit', which comes from the Latin *consuetudinem*, meaning 'custom'.

Fashion. This word appropriately entered English from French, during the Middle English period, when Middle French *façon* became Middle English *facioun* and *fasoun*. This developed into 'fasshyon' and later 'fashion'. The earlier Old French form had been *fazon*, from the Latin *facere*, meaning 'to make'. The word was first used in its current meaning in the sixteenth century as a special way of making clothes, according to the style of specific countries, and one of

Johnson's definitions (1790), 'the make or cut of cloaths', uses Shakespeare as its authority.

Barclay (1824) explained the development of the meaning from *facere* in this way: 'Fashion rises from labour, and results from the workmanship, the workman enriching it more or less according to his taste.'

Flannel. Flannel, which occurs in various forms in the Celtic languages, indicating that it may have been around for a long time, possibly entered English from the Welsh *gwlan*, meaning 'wool' during the Middle Ages; certainly by the sixteenth century the word was used for a kind of woollen cloth made in Wales, and it was still sufficiently connected to Wales for Shakespeare to use it as slang for 'Welshman'. The word has been borrowed by French, Spanish, Dutch and German, indicating the role of the cloth as a trade item. By the nineteenth century someone could be 'flannelled', i.e. washed with a piece of flannel; hence we arrive at a 'piece of cotton cloth', made in imitation of woollen flannel, used for washing.

Fur. There seems not to have been a word for 'fur' in Old English, only words for clothing made of fur. The first documentation we have for a Middle English word specifically for 'fur' while on an animal is for 'the hair on a sheep', long after there were words to do with garments made of fur or words for trimming fur for garments. Similar words in other languages of the time are to do with containing: Old and Middle French *fuerre*, meaning 'sheath or container', Middle High German *fuoter*, meaning the 'lining of a coat', and Gothic *fodr*, which means the 'sheath of a sword'. This may lead back to the root word in Sanskrit, *patra*, meaning 'container'.

Glamour. *Gramorye* or *gramorie* was an alternative form of the word 'grammar' in late Middle English, and it developed the sense of 'specialist' and then 'occult learning'. Partridge rationalises this as the idea of 'powers attributed to the learned'. Walter Scott in 1830 noted that 'the glamour', as it had developed in eighteenth-century Scotland, was a particular kind of magic, often attributed to gipsies, called *deceptio visus*, or an optical illusion; during this period the *gr* changed to *gl* to give the word 'glamer' or 'glamor', which later became 'glamour'. While during the nineteenth century the sense of visual enchantment grew more towards the idea of physical beauty attached to a scene or person, it was not until the 1930s, and possibly the influence of cinema, that 'glamour' was used for an idea of 'superficial beauty'.

Model. As a 'person who displays clothes', 'model' dates from around 1900, but Webster set out the main meanings with clarity and brevity: 'a pattern, a mould (or mold), an example, a standard, something to be copied, something to be imitated, a representation'. The 'model' as 'mould' leads us to the Italian derivation of the word, *modello*, meaning a 'wooden form' from which a mould could be taken for making metal copies. At this point the word was also linked to 'module', which in the sixteenth century carried the meanings of a 'small-scale representation or plan of something'. Cawdrey in 1604 gave the definition of 'model' as 'measure', so brief as not to be of much help. 'Model' developed into the idea of an 'original from which copies could be made', and ultimately to the copies themselves. 'To model' thus came to mean 'to act as an original for an artist to make representations from', or 'to wear clothes as an example of how prospective purchasers would look', or at least aspire to look.

Muslin. Though the word is close to 'Muslim', the connection is coincidental. 'Muslin' was adopted in the seventeenth century from the French *mousseline*, itself from the Italian *mussolina*. The word comes from Mosul, or al-Mawsil, now the second largest city in Iraq, where the cloth was originally made and exported. The spellings 'muzlin' and 'muslings' were used in the seventeenth and early eighteenth centuries, and the forms 'muslina' and 'mussolin' have been recorded.

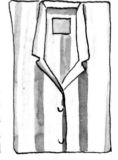

Pyjamas. Usually spelt 'pajamas' in American English, this word comes from British involvement with India, being a transcription of the Hindi *pae-jama*, meaning 'leg-clothing'. In 1828 the word was spelt more like the original, as 'paee-jams', but by the 1880s it had become 'pajama' or 'pyjamas'. The reason for the word becoming plural in English may be due to association with trousers, pants, etc. The first recorded spelling in English is in 1800 as 'pai jamahs', in an inventory of Tippoo (or Tippu) Sultan's captured wardrobe.

Silk. 'Silk' is supposed by some to have been an early introduction by Christian missionaries to England, possibly before AD 500, and as such would be an adoption directly from Latin. The original derivation is supposed to be from the Greek *seres*, the word for the people (possibly Chinese, but more likely traders further along the line) from whom the material was obtained. This word became the Latin *sericus*; and the change of the *r* to the *l* in the middle of the word is what provides the doubt about the route of the word through Europe. The *l* is there in Russian and Scandinavian language words for 'silk', proposing a Baltic trade route rather than a Christian missionary route. It appears in Old English as *sioloc* or *seoloc*, and gradually the *o* disappeared to give *silc* and *silk* by the fourteenth century.

Environment and Weather

Arctic. The Pole Star, positioned nearly over the North Pole, lies within the constellation of the Little Bear, and the 'Arctic' derives its name from this, the Greek name for 'bear' being *arktos*. The Latin names for the two bear constellations, Ursa Major and Ursa Minor, show *arktos* changing to *ursa*; however, Latin retained the form for the adjective *arcticus* and *articus*. This became Old French *artique* and Middle French *arctique*. Middle English adopted the first of these, as *artic*, with variations *artik* and *artick*, and the spelling 'Arctic' developed as scholars chose to refer back to Latin for authoritative spellings of words.

Breeze. Spelt 'brieze' in Skinner, but 'breeze' in Bailey in the same period (mid-eighteenth century), this word has changed its meaning significantly. In the sixteenth century it meant specifically the 'north or north-east wind', probably via French *brise* from similar words in Spanish and Portuguese meaning 'north-east wind', and the Italian *brezza* meaning 'cold wind', though there may be a link to Boreas, the Greek name for the 'north wind'. It was later applied to a 'cool wind on tropical coasts', and in the eighteenth century it came to mean a 'light wind'. Webster in 1828 defined 'breeze' as 'a light wind; a gentle gale', though he had to admit that 'the sense of this word (gale) is very indefinite' (see **gale**). Around the same time, Barclay's *Dictionary* defined 'breeze' as 'a gentle cooling, pleasant breath of wind'.

Cloud. Among the obsolete meanings of 'cloud' are 'hill' and 'lump of earth', showing that 'cloud' and 'clod' are related. The Old

English and Middle English spellings of *clud* and *clod* show this link, but not the breadth of overlapping meanings, for, at the same time as meaning something solid and heavy, the word was used, in the fourteenth century, for 'water vapour in the sky', and even for figurative usage based on the current use of 'cloud'. Thus in Wycliffe's *Bible* (1388) a prayer goes up to the *clowdis*, while the *OED* quotes a 1460 text which includes *clowdys of clay*, though by this time the word *clod* was being used more for 'lumps of earth'. In the early twentieth century the Cheshire and Derbyshire dialect still used 'cloud' for 'hill', but the embracing meaning of a mass congealed together is perhaps at its most startling in Johnson's description of 'fish congealed in clods of ice in winter'. Webster gave a succinct summary of the idea behind the meanings: 'I have not found this word in any other language. The sense is obvious – a collection.'

Crag. It is noteworthy that, with the exception of place-names, in common speech we use more words that have entered English from pre-Columbian America than Celtic words that survived the Anglo-Saxon invasions and the establishment of English as a language. Johnson identified 'crag' as British, that is, dating from before the period of the Anglo-Saxons; similar words for 'rock' or 'rocky place' occur in all the Celtic languages. Possibly the survival of this word gives an indication of the relationship between the Celts and the continental settlers; the fact that it is the word for a rock rather than a meadow seems appropriate. Perhaps the survival of this word gives some indication of the fate of the Celtic language in England – only two inscriptions in Celtic survived the Roman period, and only place-names and a handful of other words, mostly to do with the land, survived the migrations from the Continent.

Farm. A 'farm', meaning an 'established tract of land used for agriculture', dates only from the sixteenth century. The Middle English *ferme* meant 'lease or rent', deriving from the Middle French *fermer*, meaning 'to make a firm agreement', or 'to close a deal' (Modern French *fermer* means 'to close'). Before this, the term was applied to a fixed payment made to the Exchequer by a town or a person, which would be retrieved through taxation. Thus a 'farmer' was someone who paid a fixed amount for the right to collect taxes a hundred years before farmers 'cultivated ground' (Johnson).

Field. Bailey gave the Old English *feld* as the origin of 'field'. The vowel sound has changed considerably over the past thousand years, reflected in the different spellings *feld*, *fald*, *fild* and *feeld*, while southern pronunciation for a period in Middle English used a *v* sound at the beginning of the word (a link to the Dutch *veld*). The spelling 'fielde' emerged in the sixteenth century. Some etymologists make a link to the Old Norse *fold* and Old English *folde*, meaning 'earth', and some take it back further to Greek *platus*, meaning 'flat'.

Gale. Webster traced 'gale' back to the Danish *gal* and the Irish *gal*, from two widely separated languages; appropriately he admitted that the meaning of 'gale' could be qualified to indicate widely differing phenomena. The word has puzzled etymologists, who have offered such speculative derivations as the Icelandic *galinn*, meaning 'furious' (Skeat), the Breton Celtic *awel* meaning 'wind' (Bailey), and the Old English *galan*, from the Old Norse *gala*, meaning 'to sing' (Partridge). Around the mid-sixteenth century the word 'gaile' was being used to mean a 'storm at sea'.

Island. Few spellings taxed the patience of Noah Webster as much as that of 'island', which he declared to be 'an absurd compound of "isle" and "land"', saying 'there is no such legitimate word in English'. The trouble was that the word is a compound of two words, both meaning 'island'. The Old English *igland*, probably from the Frisian *iegland*, meant 'isle' and 'land', or 'land that is an isle'; this developed into the Middle English 'iland' or 'yland', meaning 'island'. In the fifteenth century the first part of the word became associated with the word *ile* or *yle* or *ysle*, which had developed separately from the French 'isle', from the Latin *insula*, meaning 'island'. Thus late Middle English had two words

— 34 —

– *ile* and *iland*. Latin-influenced spelling reform changed *ile* to 'isle', and this spelling influenced the spelling of 'iland', which became established as 'island' during the course of the seventeenth century.

River. The word 'river' probably derives ultimately from a Greek word *rhein*, meaning 'to flow', which probably provided a root *ri-*, which appeared in two Latin words, *ripa*, meaning 'bank or shore', and *riuus*, meaning 'stream'. These two words have provided many Modern English words, including 'arrive' in the sense of 'come to a riverbank'; 'rivulet', meaning 'a small river'; 'rivals', meaning 'inhabitants of the opposite side'; and 'derive', meaning 'to flow from'. The word was adopted from the Old French *riviere, reviere* or *rivere*, as *rivere* or *river*, taking on its modern sense from the twelfth century.

Scenery. A 'scenario', a development from the French and Italian *scena*, meaning a 'part of a performed work, etc.', was the plot of a play, ballet, masque, etc.; this was anglicised to 'scenary', which in Johnson's *Dictionary* is both the plot and a representation of where the action takes place. During the later eighteenth century the spelling changed to 'scenery' and, while the theatrical usage of 'scenery' remained, the word also came to mean a pictorial (picturesque) way of looking at a place, almost as if it were the background for theatrical action. The root word for all these is the Greek *skene*, meaning 'tent, stage or theatre building'.

Faith and Ideas

Angel. The Old English word *engel* was taken directly from the Latin *angelus*, brought to England in the sixth or seventh century by missionaries in the early period of the conversion to Christianity. The quip *Non Angli sed angeli* ('Not Angles but angels') attributed to Pope Gregory the Great in 573 when he saw some Anglo-Saxon children being sold as slaves would probably have made little sense to the objects of his interest: the plural of *engel* was *englas*, while the word for Angles might have been *Angle* or *Engle,* but more likely would have depended on what part of the land they came from. The Latin word derived from the Greek *angelos*, 'messenger', which itself may have a connection to an ancient Persian word for 'messenger or courier'. The modern spelling has been in use since the time of Shakespeare.

Chapel. One theory proposes that the word 'chapel' derived from the place where the 'cape' of St Martin of Tours was preserved. Wedgwood thought a more satisfactory derivation would come from turning this round, that a 'cover or hood' over a relic might develop into a reliquary and then into a 'chapel'. The *OED* supports the idea that the relic gave its name to the place it was kept in, and thus to any sacred place for storing relics, and then to a 'small consecrated place'. There is some confusion over two words, the Vulgar Latin *cappella*, itself conjectural, meaning 'short cloak', and the Medieval Latin *capella*, meaning 'chapel'; each of these has been used to support the differing etymologies. Either way, the word *chapele* arrived in Middle English in the thirteenth century but was not fully established as 'chapel' until the nineteenth century.

Conscience. In the fourteenth century the early forms of 'conscience' took over from the Middle English word *inwit*, and the earliest recorded use shows this happening, in 1225: 'ure owune conscience, thet is, ure inwit' (*OED*). *Inwit* is a simple and clear word, giving an idea of knowing something deep inside, almost an animal instinct; William Barnes tried to reinstate it in the nineteenth century. Often the final *s* sound of 'conscience', which in Latin means literally 'with-knowing', seems to have given a sense of the word referring to something plural. The *OED* cites illiterate spellings 'consions' and 'conchons' as having to render something like the plural sense of 'wits' or 'brains', as in 'lost your wits'.

Cross. The Old English word for the Christian cross was *rod*, which still survives in the word 'rood' applied to the rood-screen in some old churches. The word 'cross' derives from the Latin *crux*, which travelled with missionaries from Rome throughout Europe, appearing in Old Norse as *kross*. *Cros* appeared in England in the tenth century as a place-name in Cambridgeshire, *Normannes cros*, followed by other place-names in northern England. This led to supposition that it might be a Viking introduction; against expectation, evidence and documentation indicate that many Vikings had contact with and converted to Christianity from the ninth century. It is also possible that the word entered as an introduction by Celtic missionaries from Ireland, the Latin word having entered Old Irish as *cros* (the Modern Welsh word is *croes*). At the Battle of Hastings, the English battle-cry was 'Olicrosse' (Holy Cross, from the name of the church at Waltham Abbey), but after the Conquest the word was reintroduced from Norman French, as *croiz, crois* and *croys,* and later *croice*, which dominated in the south; but these forms died out in the fifteenth century, leaving the older form, which had survived in the north, dominant. The spelling 'cross' became established in the seventeenth century.

Ghost. Early missionaries to England took over the Old English word *gast*, meaning 'demon', an echo of which remains in the word 'ghastly', and used it for the Christian concepts of the soul and the Holy Ghost. The Middle English period saw variations in the spelling, including *gost, gast* and *goost*, but the major change in spelling arrived when Caxton spelled it with *gh-*. It is claimed that Caxton was influenced by the Flemish word *gheest* (Caxton had been a printer in Bruges before setting up England's first press, in 1476); Partridge blames the intrusive *h* entirely on Caxton's compositors. The prevailing sense, that of 'the manifest spirit of a dead person', dates back to Chaucer in the fourteenth century.

Hopefully. Despite being the *bête noire* of many self-styled guardians of English, 'hopefully' has been used in the sense of 'I hope' for a long time. The online *Merriam-Webster Dictionary* dates this usage back to the eighteenth century, with common usage dating back to the 1930s. The use of the word in this way is similar to the use of words like 'frankly' or 'curiously', so it should not cause distress, especially as both its intonation when spoken and the position of the word in a sentence act to differentiate it from the sense of 'with hope'.

'Hope' comes from *tohopa*, which appeared in Old Low German and spread to Scandinavian languages, arriving in Old English as the noun *hopa*, and the corresponding verb *hopian*. These became *hope* in the thirteenth century, and remained so, with a few spelling variations, 'hoope', 'howp' and 'houp', in the fifteenth and sixteenth centuries.

Paradise. 'Paradise' was adopted in the Middle English period from the Greek *paradeisos* via Late Latin and Old French. The Old Iranian words *pari* and *daez*, meaning 'to build around' had given the word *pairidaeza*, meaning 'nobleman's garden', and this had links to the Hebrew *pardes*, meaning an 'enclosed garden', particularly those of the Persian kings. The Greek word was used to describe a 'Persian enclosed pleasure garden' at the time of Alexander the Great, around 330 BC, and was adopted for both the Christian word for 'heaven', the place where blessed souls wait for resurrection and the Garden of Eden.

Prayer. This is a word in which the spelling at first kept up with changes in pronunciation but seems to have been fixed at the time of the increase in printing in the early seventeenth century. The Late Latin word *precaria*, meaning 'entreaty or request', lost the letter *c* when it became the Old French *preiere*, and this was shortened to the Middle French and Anglo-Norman *priere*. In Anglo-Norman this developed into the forms *praere*, *praiere* and *preire*, which were adopted into Middle English. During the next four centuries the *-eier* and *-eyer* spellings changed to *-aier* and *-ayer*, leaving us with the curious spelling we have today.

Solemn. 'Solemn' derives from a sequence of terms to do with religious ritual. The Latin *solemnis* was a variant of *sollennis*, meaning 'performed ritualistically or in careful detail', which developed the meaning of 'annual' or 'regular' (though 'annual' was more likely to be a development of the sense of 'regular' than a link to the Latin word *annus*, meaning 'year'); the root word for these was *sollus*, meaning 'whole' or 'complete'. In Late Latin these gave rise to *solemnizare*, meaning 'to celebrate a ritual or rite of worship', and *solemnis*, which developed into Old and Middle French *solempne* and *solemne*. Middle English adopted both these forms, but by about 1550 the variant with *p* had disappeared.

Synagogue. 'The house of the ruler of the synagogue' appears as the wording in the 1611 translation of the Bible, though few British people at that time would have seen a synagogue. In the Wessex Gospels, a 990 translation, the phrase is rendered as 'heah-ealdres hus', which would indicate the absence of a word for 'synagogue' in Old English. Two Greek roots meaning 'lead' and 'together' became the Latin *synagoga* and the Old French *synagogue*; this was in use as *sinagoge* before the Jews were expelled from England in 1290. Around 1290 too is the first documented use of the current spelling. The form 'synagog' has been an accepted variant spelling in America but did not originate with Webster; *Pollard's Advanced Speller*, published in 1897, promoted the American Philological Association's recommendation to drop the *-ue* suffix to reform the spelling of such words as 'demagog', 'epilog' and 'synagog', but the last of these does not get past a current American Microsoft spellchecker program.

Family and People

Bachelor. This word puzzled many of the early dictionary writers; suggestions for its source include the Greek word for 'foolish', the Celtic word for 'little', the French words *bas chevalier*, meaning the 'lowest rank of knighthood', the 'holder of a small estate' (*baccalarius* in Late Latin), the French word for 'cow-herd', and even a contraction of 'bag-age-caller', i.e. a 'young scholar' (Lemon, 1783). Johnson suggested *bacca laura*, the berry of the laurel or bay, saying 'batchelors are spare of good hopes like laurels in the berry'; while Webster preferred the Latin *baculus*, meaning 'stick or shoot'. Even the *OED* states that there is uncertainty about the etymology, and thus the developments of meaning. The first recorded use of the word specifically for an unmarried man comes in Chaucer, in 1386.

Bridegroom. Few words provoked Webster's impatience about improper spelling more than 'bridegroom'. In the 1832 edition of his *Dictionary* he claimed it should be 'properly bridegoom', in accordance with its Old English form, *brydguma*, a combination of 'bride' and a poetic word for 'man'. *Guma* probably came from the same root as the Latin *homo*, meaning 'man'. The form 'brydegrome' appeared in the early sixteenth century, by which time *guma* or *gome* had become obsolete. It is likely that the change from 'gome' to 'groom' occurred by association with the word 'groom', meaning 'young man or servant'. The current spelling

is that recommended by Mulcaster in his list of spellings in *The Elementarie* in 1582.

Brother. The Old English *brothor* or *brother* can be found in the *Anglo-Saxon Chronicle* for 656. The conjectural root in Indo-European is *bhrat*, which lies behind words for 'brother' in most languages from Lithuanian (*brolis*) to Sanskrit (*bhratr*). The variety of forms for the plural in Middle English included *brothre*, *brotherne*, *brotheren* and *brethren*. 'Brothers' is recorded as the plural only once before Shakespeare, where it is used equally with 'brethren', which gradually became limited to ecclesiastical use. Isidore of Seville proposed that the Latin *frater*, which comes from the Greek word with the same sound, derived from the Latin *fructus*, meaning 'fruit', as your brother is effectively 'seed of the same womb'.

Father. The root of this word lies way back in Indo-European, as can be seen from the similarity in words for 'father' across a wide range of languages, from the Sanskrit *pitr* to the Old Norse *fadir*; Johnson noted that a similar word existed in Persian. Partridge linked the Latin form, *pater*, to many English words with a sense of 'what lies behind or above: pattern, repair, Jupiter, patriot'. The *d* for the central consonant was retained from Old English *fader* until the sixteenth century, though it is mostly accepted that the sound was softened to *th* over a hundred years previously, while in southern Middle English during the thirteenth and fourteenth centuries the opening consonant sound was spelt with a *v*.

Girl. Johnson wrote: 'About the etymology of this word there is much question.' Webster's idea that it derives from a Latin word for 'servant' and survived through the Old English period has been joined by theories that it derives from words for a kind of dress, a child, a rose-blossom, and from a supposedly lost word for 'woman'. What can be said is that the word was used in the fourteenth and fifteenth centuries for a 'child of either sex' and did not become established as a counterpart to 'boy' until the sixteenth century. It is perhaps surprising that such a straightforward idea (for us) should not have had a single clear word that could be traced back through several centuries, but the *OED* points out that the etymology is difficult also for 'boy', 'lad' and 'lass'. 'Child', however, has remained constant for over a thousand years and can be traced back to the Hebrew of the Old Testament.

Husband. This word was an early Scandinavian adoption, the word *husbonda* meaning a 'householder', literally a 'house-freeman'. The word 'husbandman', as one who works on the land, retains something of this meaning, as does the verb 'to husband', as in 'to husband one's resources'. In northern dialects of English the word meant a 'tenant of the manor', corresponding to the word 'villein' elsewhere. These early uses were thus not gender specific, and Serjeantson gives a feminine form of the word found in Ælfric's *Heptateuch* of the eleventh century. The first use of the word as a counterpart to 'wife' was in the thirteenth century.

Lady. The words 'lord' and 'lady' indicate in their histories the importance that bread had in the Anglo-Saxon household. 'Lady' is derived from the Old English *hlaf*, meaning 'bread', and *dige*, 'one who kneads', from a Germanic root meaning 'to knead or dig'. The process by which this household task developed into the word for a 'female person of rank' probably had something to do with providing or controlling food. Certainly its counterpart, *hlaford*, which became 'lord', meant 'controller of bread'. *Hlafdige*, around the year 850, was used in an Old English translation of the Psalms for the Latin *domina*, meaning 'mistress', and was applied to the consort of the kings of Wessex, in preference to *cwen*, the word for 'queen', and by the early thirteenth century it was being applied to the Virgin Mary. The word changed to *hlafdi* towards the end of the Old English period, and during the thirteenth and fourteenth centuries the *f* became *v* and eventually disappeared.

Nephew. The Latin term *fratris filius* specified 'son of a sibling', while *nepos* meant 'grandson or descendant', and this sense carried on into the Old and Middle French *neveu*, which in turn became the Anglo-Norman *neveu* or *nevou*. However, the range of words such as Old Persian *napa* and Sanskrit *napat*, meaning 'grandson', and Old Norse *nefi* and Irish *nia*, meaning 'nephew', indicate an Indo-European root for a male blood-relative. When the word was adopted into Middle English it gave rise to a vast range of spellings; the *OED* lists thirty-four in the Middle English period alone, including *neveaw*, *newof* and *neuo*. The development of the spelling of the middle consonant is something of a mystery: though there are a few documented uses of the *ph* spelling in the word before 1550, there is no *ph* spelling in a Latin-from-Greek root word that would account for this. It is possible that it became established through what Donald Scragg calls the 'extreme sensitivity to Latin [and by extension Greek] on the part of writers of English'. The pronunciation of the middle consonant as in the word 'off' has largely superseded the earlier pronunciation as in the word 'of', but this was a long process. Both pronunciations were given in the 1861 *Chambers Dictionary* and the 1908 *OED*, but in 1974 Scragg wrote that the *v* sound 'is changing to *f* in present day English', and attributed this to pronunciation following spelling, against the usual pattern.

Niece. The Late Latin *neptis* had a feminine form *nepta*, which developed into *neptia* in Vulgar Latin, and then to *niéce* in Old French, and *niece* in Anglo-Norman. As with 'nephew', the word also meant 'granddaughter' and 'female relative', these usages now being obsolete. Between the fourteenth and seventeenth centuries the word was applied also to male relatives, a usage which was maintained longer in the United States and in the twentieth century was still in use in this sense among African Americans.

Person. The idea of 'person', as in 'personal' or 'in person', as a tangible presence is at odds with its root meaning in Latin, from Greek, of the 'mask used by an actor'. In Middle English 'person', or 'parson', had the meaning both of 'someone in a specified role' and 'the body of that person'. Shakespeare used both meanings, of portraying and being, in the phrases 'the person of Moonshine' (*A Midsummer Night's Dream*) and 'her own person' (*Antony and Cleopatra*). The word 'impersonate' carries both meanings.

Sister. Wedgwood noted that many Indo-European languages have words similar to 'sister' for the same relationship: *seostra* in Polish, *sossar* and *sessu* in Estonian, *swastri* and *sodary* in Sanskrit. To these Partridge adds Old Frisian *swester*, the Old Saxon *swestar* and the Old English *sweoster*, and he notes that for most of the old Germanic languages the word begins *sw-*. This indicates that the Middle and

Modern English derives not from a southern Germanic root but from the Old Norse form *syster*. In all the other words for relationships within a nuclear family group the development has been direct from the Old English word; it is not known why the Old Norse *syster* supplanted the Old English *sweoster*.

Son. The earliest recorded spelling of 'son' in Old English is *sunu*, from about 825, and the same spelling occurs in Old Saxon, Old Frisian and Old High German, indicating a common Germanic root for the word. Similar forms appear in Lithuanian, Russian, Old Slavonic and Sanskrit. The spelling of the vowel sound was maintained until the fourteenth century, when the spellings *soone, soonne, soon* and *soun(e)* appeared, alongside *son*. The Latin root for 'son', *filius*, did not supplant the Old English word but did provide the word 'filial', and, according to Partridge, 'affiliate'.

Stepmother. Old English had words for all family relationships devolving from a second marriage, using the prefix *steop-*, from *astepan* and *astypan*, meaning 'to bereave'. The word *steopmoder* can be found in an early eighth-century document and appears from a comment by Johnson to have been the only step-relationship in continuous use since then. It is also the catalyst for some of his ironic word-play: 'as it is now seldom applied but to the mother it seems to mean in the mind of those who use it, a woman who has stepped into the vacant place of the true mother.'

Woman. The plural spelling of 'women' obviously annoyed Noah Webster, who wrote: 'The plural as written, seems to be "womb-men". But we pronounce it *wimen*, and so it ought to be written'; but the *OED* shows this to be have been just about the only spelling of the plural never to have been used. The Old English *wifman* (plural *wifmen*) developed into the Middle English *wimman* and *wimmen*; during the period 1200 to 1300 these developed into *womman* and *wommen*, and then the simplified spellings of 'woman' and 'women', which became the regular forms around 1400. By analogy with singular/plural forms like 'tooth/teeth', the first vowels of both words developed into the pronunciations we have today. The early Old English word for 'woman' was *wif*, which survives in words such as 'fishwife'.

Food and Drink

Bistro. One explanation for this word is that it is the Russian *bystro*, meaning 'quick', which entered English from French by a curious route. Either French soldiers in Russia during the Napoleonic Wars picked up the word at cafés and restaurants there, demanding quick service, or Russian soldiers in Paris after the fall of Napoleon used the word in a similar way there. Conceivably the word entered French by both routes. Another explanation is that the word comes from *bistouille*, French for 'cheap wine', or *bistrouille*, French for 'brandy mixed with coffee'. It is not recorded in English until the 1920s.

Blancmange. This word was borrowed from French twice, from the Normans as *blankmanger*, a dish of poultry mixed with cream, eggs and other ingredients, and in the later eighteenth century as 'blomange', as a dessert. The spelling of the second borrowing evidently followed the pronunciation, and the 'correct spelling', a direct translation of 'white eat', developed around 1800, as both 'blanc-manger' and 'blancmange'. The *OED* describes the later spelling as 'a half-attempt at restoring the French, but the pronunciation is that of the 18th century "blomange", "blamange", etc, often garnished with a French nasal, by those who know French'.

Breakfast. When we breakfast we 'break a fast', that is we 'desist from not eating'. The old word for 'breakfast', which has disappeared, was 'ientation', which Cawdrey in 1604 defined as 'breakefast'. Later in the century, Cockeram's *Dictionary* included 'to Breakfast — Ienticulate'; and 'Jenticulation — a breaking ones fast'.

These wonderful words, coming from the Latin *ientaculum*, meaning 'breakfast', seem to describe a meal far more elaborate and positive than the curious double negative of not not eating, which is first recorded from 1463 (*OED*).

Coffee. 'Coffee' seems to have managed to retain a connection to the location where it was first grown, reputedly the area of Kaffa in Ethiopia, where the plant is indigenous. However, it was the drink and not the plant or the bean that acquired the Arabic name *qahwah*; cultivation of the plant spread to Turkey, becoming *kahveh*, and it was from here that 'coffee' started to spread to Europe in about 1600. The first nation and language to adopt the taste was Italian, and while some languages, Italian, French, Spanish, Portuguese, German, Danish and Swedish, retained the short *a* for the first vowel, English was among those which changed it to a short *o*. In the early seventeenth century English writers used a diversity of spellings, including 'cahve', 'coffee', 'coffa', 'caffa', 'capha', 'cauphe', 'cophic', 'cophee', 'coffe', and 'coffey'. To these may be added another spelling, for the scientific name for the genus is 'Coffea'.

Egg. In one of the first books to be printed in England, Caxton's translation of the *Aeneid* in 1490, there is a story about some sailors in the Thames estuary who came ashore to get food. One of them, called Sheffield, asked a local woman if they could buy some eggs, but she replied angrily that she could not speak French. Of course, 'eggs' is not a French word, but the point is that as late as 1490 the northern dialect word ('eggs') could sound as foreign as French to someone in the south, for whom the word would have been *eyren*.

As a printer, Caxton had to decide which form he was going to use. In this case the northern form, from the Old Norse *egg*, won out over the southern, Germanic form, *ey(e)* and *ay(e)*. Webster thought the etymology was from the Latin *ovum*, with the *v* changing to a *g*, which may be far-fetched, but Partridge takes it back further to the Greek word *oïon*, which may be the root for the Latin, Germanic and Scandinavian forms.

Flour. In his 1755 *Dictionary* Johnson did not have 'flour' as a separate entry, including it within 'flower', though the two were by then diverging into entirely different words. The connection is that 'flour' was understood to be the 'flower' of the grain, the best part, (as in the expression 'the flower of chivalry'). The Middle French expression *flour de farine* provided Middle English with *flure* or *flour*. Though the spelling 'flour' for 'ground grain' was used in the fourteenth century, 'flower' persisted until the early nineteenth century. To confuse matters further, Wycliffe's Bible spelled 'the blossom of a plant' as *flour* in 1382; and the translation of the Latin root *florere*, now spelt as 'to flourish', shows that the connection between the two persists.

Greengage. Sir William Gage in 1724 planted in his garden in Bury St Edmunds the seeds of a new variety of plum imported from France. Reputedly the labels were lost in transit, and the fruit became known in English as 'greengage', on account of its colour, though until the early nineteenth century they were also called 'Green Gage Plums'. In France they have been long known as 'Reine Claude', after the queen of François I.

Hamburger. 'Hamburgers' have nothing to do with ham but were steaks cooked in a way that had some kind of connection to Hamburg. But interpretation of the nature of that connection differs. Some authorities state that the cooking method travelled to North America with German émigrés during the mid-nineteenth century and was not specifically related to Hamburg. Two sources concur on a more precise story. Theodora Fitzgibbon and Giovanni Ballarini propose that the food, and thus its name, originated on the Hamburg steamer line, which took migrants from Hamburg to America in the 1850s, and that the food was merely a quick way of cooking steak on board. During the First World War 'hamburgers' were renamed 'Salisbury steaks', as part of the process of anglicising items with German names.

Jam. There is little consensus about 'jam'. Johnson delightfully thought that 'jam' came from French children saying '*j'aime*', meaning 'I like it'. Wedgwood was not impressed with Skeat's idea of it coming from the word 'champ', meaning 'to bite or chew noisily', and proposed that it came from the word 'jamb', the upright part of a door-frame, as closing a door involves pressing it between the jambs (presumably he had rather close-fitting doors). Partridge goes with the idea of something produced by pressing, so coming from the word 'champ' (as horses champ at the bit); this word previously had the form 'cham'. Many early dictionary writers ended up like James Barclay, writing 'etymology unknown'.

As food, the word is first documented in Bailey's *Dictionary* in 1736, with the same etymology as Johnson's. The idea of things, people or cars pressed together was early on spelt 'jamb', supporting Wedgwood's idea, though Robinson Crusoe's ship was 'stuck fast, jaum'd in between two Rocks' in 1719.

Marmalade. Despite the appeal of the story of 'marmalade' being originally *Marie malade*, a fruit conserve made for Mary, Queen of Scots, while she was ill as a child at the court of France, 'marmalade' arrived in late Middle English a hundred years earlier, in the late fifteenth century. Its origin is seen in Johnson's definition, 'the pulp of quinces boiled into a consistence with sugar', for the Portuguese *marmelada* came from *marmelo*, meaning 'quince', from the Latin *malomellum*. Isidore connected the quince or 'sweet apple' called *malomellum* with *mel*, 'honey', because it either tasted sweet or was served with honey.

Meat. There are still a few expressions that carry the meaning of 'meat' as 'any solid food', 'meat' as opposed to 'drink'. It was only from the fourteenth century that the word was applied specifically to 'flesh' and in some usages is kept distinct from 'fish'. Forms similar to the present spelling are to be found in Old English and several other Germanic languages, as well as Celtic languages, for example Old Irish *maisse*, as well as the Sanskrit word *medas*, meaning 'fat'; these indicate an Indo-European root *mad-*, which can be seen in the Latin word *madere*, meaning 'to be succulent'.

Mustard. The Old English word for mustard, *sinop*, from the Latin *sinapis*, was replaced by a word from Latin via Old French, deriving from the process of making mustard ready for the table, rather than from the plant itself. The difference in status between Norman and Saxon was reflected in the language of food, often producing two words, for the cooked and uncooked food; pork/pig, mutton/sheep and beef/cow are well known, but this distinction extended to other foods, and indeed all round the house, producing 'chair/stool', 'chamber/room' and 'mansion/house'. Mustard ground with vinegar, also known as 'must' (Latin *mustum*), produced the sauce called in Old French *moustarde* or *moutarde*. The first documented appearance of 'mostard' in English was in some household expenses of 1289; during the fourteenth century 'mostard' became 'mustard'. The idea that the phrase 'as keen as mustard' was invented to advertise Keen's Mustard is sadly untrue; the phrase was recorded in 1672, decades before the founding of the company.

Onion. The *OED* lists thirty-three different spellings for 'onion' in the Middle English period alone, and the total list including regional and American spellings runs to over a hundred. There were several variant spellings for the Anglo-Norman word, including *ungeon*, *hunnun*, *oynoin* and *ognon*, as well as *uniun*; this last is a link to the Late Latin *unio*, deriving from *unus*, meaning 'one', which was used to describe both a 'large pearl' and a 'single-shooting onion'. The Normans did not introduce the vegetable; the Old English *ciepe* was an early acquisition from the Latin *cepa*, meaning 'onion'. But the Anglo-Norman word squeezed out the English one, leaving 'onions' with a permanent association with France.

Pea. The Old English word was *piose*, which had a form *piosan* to describe both the plural and the collective. These developed two strands for the plural, one ending in *s* and the other in *n*, through

Middle English up to the eighteenth century; in most cases the spellings were variations on *peese* or *pease* – Mulcaster uncharacteristically confuses the issue by offering three alternative spellings, 'peace', 'peach' and 'pease'. In late Middle English the plural and singular were identical, which gave rise to the invention of a new singular, the word 'pea'. By the mid-seventeenth century the old collective and plural form had become identical with the new plural, 'peas'. The plural form 'peas' still exists alongside the collective form 'pease', which can be found in several compound words, such as 'peasemeal', 'peasecod' and 'peaseblossom'. The word was acquired by Germanic people from the Latin *pisum*, before they began to migrate to England in the sixth century.

Potato. Serjeantson quotes Sir John Hawkins in *The Voyage to Florida* (1565) describing potatoes as 'the most delicate rootes that may be eaten', and thus using the word for the first time in English. He was describing the sweet potato, *Ipomoea batatas*, which was described by the English herbalist Gerard in 1597 as 'potatoes or the common potatoes', with variant spellings 'potatus' and 'potades'. This word derived from the Spanish adoption of the Haitian word *batata*, following Columbus's introduction of the plant to Spain after his first voyage. This was not the *Solanum tuberosum*, which we now know as 'potato', but which was at first called in English 'Virginia potato'. This plant was taken by the Spanish in the 1530s from the Peruvian Andes first to the Canaries and then to mainland Europe; its local Quechua name was *papas*, still retained in colloquial Spanish. Variations on the word *batata* seem to have been applied to a number of New World tuberous vegetables, but 'potato' has stuck to the two most commonly eaten species.

Spam. In 1937 a new canned meat was marketed by the American company George A. Hormel of Austin, Minnesota. As the meat was from the shoulder rather than the leg of pork, it could not be called 'ham', but the president of the company found a novel way of finding a new name. He threw a large party at which the meat was served, but for the guests the price of a drink was a suggestion of a name for the new product. It was here that an actor named Kenneth Daigneau suggested the word 'spam', which he claimed was a catchy trade-name he had thought of some time before; lacking an appropriate product to suggest it for, he had been saving it up. If correct, this story would indicate that the usually accepted story, that 'spam' is an abbreviation of 'spiced ham', is folk etymology, a logical but erroneous derivation.

The use of the word for 'unsolicited email' is said to derive from a *Monty Python* sketch broadcast in 1970, in which the word was repeated incessantly. Alternatively it is an acronym for 'simultaneously posted advertising message', or 'sales promotional advertising mail'.

Tea. In English the drink was originally 'tee' or 'tay', having arrived in England in the seventeenth century via the Dutch word *thee*, which had been the nearest the Europeans could get to what is now written as *t'e*, traded at Bantam in Java from Chinese merchants from the Amoy region of China. In the Mandarin and Cantonese dialects this would have been *ch'a*, which became the Portuguese *cha*, which was recorded, but not drunk, in England in 1598. The word and the drink were known in France from 1635, but not until 1650 in England. The original pronunciation, to rhyme with 'bay', can be seen through rhymes surviving till the mid-eighteenth century.

Tomato. The tomato was brought to Europe from the New World in the sixteenth century and was being cultivated by 1550 in Italy, where, for its supposed aphrodisiac properties, it was known as the 'love-apple' (Webster recorded this as an alternative name in 1828). *Tomatl* is the nearest the Europeans could get to the form of the word in Nahuatl, the indigenous language of the Aztecs in Mexico, where the plant was found by the Spanish. Another transcription from Nahuatl is *xitomatl.* The word entered Spanish and Portuguese as *tomate*, changing to 'tomato' when it entered English, being first documented in text in 1604. When Noah Webster accused his rival

Joseph Worcester of plagiarism, 'tomato' was one of the words that Webster believed had been copied from his dictionary.

Treacle. The word *theriac*, which occurs in a late Old English medical tract but not again till the sixteenth century, meant an 'antidote to poisons', especially the bite of a venomous snake. This word derived from the Latin and Greek words for 'to do with wild beasts' and provided the root for the Middle English *tryacle* or *triacle*. 'Treacle' at this time continued to have more to do with healing than sweetening and was not applied to the 'syrup of molasses' until the late seventeenth century (Johnson defined it as 'the spume of sugar'). What was later called a 'balm' was in the sixteenth century called a 'treacle', and the use of the word for anything with healing properties survived, just, into the nineteenth century. Webster's 1828 *Dictionary* includes this meaning as 'a medicinal compound of various ingredients', but the 1832 edition has 'no longer a balm'.

Garden

Bonfire. There are two strands as regards the meaning of 'bon' in 'bonfire' – 'good' and 'bone'. There was a suggestion that the word arose during the Protestant Reformation, referring to a martyr's execution, but the word was in use by 1520. The idea that 'bonfires' are often acts of celebration may lead to the idea that the word means 'good fire', the derivation that Johnson preferred. To confuse the issue further, there were in the seventeenth century public burnings of bones, which must have smelt awful. It seems likely that the word was originally 'bone-fire' (the spelling was in use until the eighteenth century) but started to change to 'bonfire' in the early seventeenth century, this becoming the dominant and eventually accepted spelling. The idea of the derivation from a word meaning 'good' is an attractive but false deduction. The 'fire' part of the word comes from the French *feu* and is related to the word 'pyre'.

Buddleia. The so called 'butterfly bush' was named by Linnaeus after the Reverend Adam Buddle, who died in 1708, having compiled an English *Flora*, which was never published. The original spelling was 'buddleja', as written by Linnaeus, which should have prevailed, as the first naming of a specimen is supposed to be definitive; but both the spellings are current in scientific nomenclature.

Compost. The Latin root words *cum* and *ponere*, meaning 'to put with', gave the Latin word *compositum*, which came into Old French with the meaning of 'mixture'; this became the fourteenth-century 'compost', meaning 'stew or preserve of fruits' (French *compôte*). The *OED* dates the application of the word to a 'soil-enriching mixture' to the 1580s, suggesting that 'to compost' had been used a hundred years earlier in the sense not of mixing ingredients together but merely of spreading manure over the soil. The evidence is inconclusive here – Caxton's 'by which dongyng and composting the feldes gladeth' (1481, *OED*) could be describing two actions or the same action in two ways. Johnson's definition describes 'compost' as both 'a mixture of various substances for enriching the ground; [and] manure'.

Daisy. The Middle English *daiseie*, which developed from the Old English *daeges eage*, leads us to the origin of the name of the flower. It is the 'day's eye', the ring of petals round the centre like an eye which opens during the day and closes at night. In the fourteenth century this meaning of the word was still clear, as Chaucer refers to 'the dayeseye, or ellis the eye of day'.

Geranium. The common name for a geranium is 'cranesbill', this being suggested by the seedcase's resemblance to the shape of the head and beak of a crane. 'Geranium' retains this visual link, as *geranos* is the Ancient Greek for a crane. The word is documented from the mid-sixteenth century.

Lawn. Lawn probably came to English from a Breton Celtic word *lann*, appearing in Middle English as *laund*, from which the last letter disappeared; the route of the etymology is disputed, but most authorities agree that it comes from words meaning 'open or uncultivated land'. However, Johnson's definition of a lawn as 'an open space between woods' links to Wedgwood's idea of a lawn as 'a grass land surrounded by trees', coming from a Norse word *glana*, meaning 'to shine or be visible through something'. This had the advantage of linking to the semi-transparent cotton cloth called 'lawn'. But it is more probable that the name of the cloth derived from Laon, to the north-west of Rheims, 'lawn' being known for some time as 'the cloth of Rheims'.

Orchard. An orchard was formerly an 'ort-yard', the spelling catching up with the pronunciation by the late Middle Ages. The 'yard' part of the word is still in use as an alternative to 'garden' for a patch of land beside a house. The first part derives from an Old English word *wort* meaning 'vegetable' or 'herb', which is still around in 'St John's wort' and many other wildflowers, 'colewort', and much changed in 'mangel-wurzel'. Sixteenth-century linguists re-analysed the word as a combination of the Latin *hortus*, 'garden', with 'yard', but this would imply a pointless repetition, though this does happen, especially in place-names – such as Hampton (literally 'village village').

Prune. 'To prune' has two meanings, one more or less obsolete and replaced by 'to preen'; this referred to birds setting their feathers in order, or to people arranging their clothes or hair, and was previously 'proin', 'proyn' or 'proign', an adoption from Anglo-Norman. It would be tempting to think that 'pruning' a tree also meant 'setting it in order', but in fact it comes from a different and older French word, *proignier*, meaning 'to prune'. Beyond that few etymologists care to go, though Partridge states that it comes from the Latin prefix *per-* connected to *rotundus*, meaning 'round', thus meaning 'to round off'. Johnson felt the meaning of 'to prune' as 'to preen' was slang, defining it as 'to dress, to prink, a ludicrous word'. 'To prink' meant 'to prank', and 'to prank' meant 'to decorate', still in use in the 1970s according to the *Chambers Twentieth Century Dictionary*.

Trellis. The Old French word *treliz* was constructed from the Latin *tri* and *licium*, meaning 'three threads', as it meant a warp (the horizontal line in a loom) made of three threads, and thus a 'strong coarse cloth'. This developed into the use of the same construction for metalwork, which appeared in late Middle English as the words *treles* or *trelys* for an 'openwork structure of crossed wood or metal bars in a window'. At the same time the Old French word *treille* or *traille,* meaning a 'bower of vine branches supported on lattice-work', from the Latin *trichila*, meaning ' bower', developed into the Middle English *treylle* or *traylle*. By the early sixteenth century these two senses, of a plant support and a lattice design, had come together in the use of a 'trailzeys' for training fruit trees against a lattice-work support, with the spelling 'trellis' developing later in the century.

Home

Attic. In the Renaissance the word 'attic' was applied to the storey directly above the cornice projecting over the entrance to a house. During the Palladian revival of the eighteenth century the 'attic' or 'attick' was a decorative device consisting of pillars and entablature (the triangular design resting on pillars), from which it developed into the whole storey, typically with pillars. By the early nineteenth century it had become merely the storey in the upper part of a house, specifically with square windows. Gradually the name came to be applied to the part of the house directly under the roof, with little or no decoration. The word comes from 'Attica', the region of Greece where Athens is located; the word appeared in English in this sense in the late sixteenth century.

Beaker. 'Beaker' comes from the Middle English *biker*, which came from the Old Norse *bikarr*. Similar words appear in other Germanic languages, and the ultimate derivation may be the early Medieval Latin *becarium*, from *baca*, meaning 'water vessel', or the Greek *bikos*, meaning 'drinking bowl'. Bailey, defining 'beaker' as having a 'spout like a bird's beak', thought it might come from 'beak'; but the use of the word for a 'glass container with a small spout for pouring', as used in chemistry experiments, is not recorded before 1877, more than a century after Bailey's dictionary. The spelling 'beaker' was recorded in 1600, but it is doubtful that, outside the laboratory, beakers ever had beaks.

Carpet. 'Carpet', both word and item, was imported from France, where it appears as the Old and Middle French word *carpite*, itself coming from the Medieval Latin word *carpita*, meaning 'woolly cloths'. The form 'carpet' was established by the sixteenth century. The less luxurious 'rug' comes from the Scandinavian words *rugga*, 'coarse rug', and Old Norse *rögg*, 'tuft'. A 'carpet' originally was a covering for a table rather than a floor and is defined as such as late as Bailey's 1727 *Dictionary.*

Cupboard. A 'cupboard' was originally a shelf, that is a 'board', for cups and other vessels. The apparent simplicity of this is confused by the first documented use of the word around 1325: 'Couered mony a cup-borde with clothes ful quite' (*OED*). The idea that a 'cupboard' was specifically intended to house drinking vessels became so obscured by use that around 1600 the 'cup' element of the word began to lose its final *p*, and spellings such as 'cubboorde', 'cubbard' and 'cubbert' appeared. In the eighteenth century the rationalisation of spelling referring to etymological roots brought the spelling back to 'cupboard', and this is how Johnson spelled it. Cockeram's *Dictionary* in 1670 contained the word 'ambrey', meaning 'cupboard', a word now limited to ecclesiastical usage.

Cushion. Unlike 'pillow', the word 'cushion' derives from the part of the body it relates to. The Latin for 'thigh' is *coax*, which developed into a form something like *coxinus*, which in turn developed into the Old French forms *coessin,* then *coissin*, and finally *coussin*. These were adopted into Middle English as *cuisshin* and *quishin*. Another form developed in Middle English as *cusshyn* or *cushin*. 'Cushions' seem to have been a fashion imported from France, bringing the distinction of not having to put your head on something you had sat on. *Whyssynes*, a northern dialect form, appears in the poem *Gawain and the Green Knight*, of about 1330, and the *OED* lists the following spellings between 1361 and 1530: *quissyn, quysshon, cuyschun, quisshen, cuysshen, quission*. Shakespeare in 1601 spelled it 'cushion'.

Drawer. From the action 'to draw', this word comes from the Middle English *drahen* and later *drawen*, from the earlier Old English *dragan* (from which we get 'to drag'). These are related to many words for the same action in other Germanic languages, and they may all derive from the Latin *trahere*, meaning 'to pull, draw, drag'. The first use of the word with the *-er* suffix for the article of furniture is in 1580.

Kettle. Isidore of Seville proposed that the Latin word for 'kettle', *cucuma*, derived from the noise of water boiling in the vessel, a reasonable idea. There is perhaps part of this in the words which fed into the word in Modern English, the Old Norse *ketill* and the Latin *catillus*, which became the Old English *cetel* and the Middle English *ketel*. During the period 1300 to 1600 a wide range of spellings are seen: *ketil, kettyll, chetyle*. But it is difficult to know when the word was applied specifically to the item we know today as a 'kettle', especially as we retain the idea of an open top in 'paint-kettle'. Johnson in 1755 defined it thus: 'the name of pot is given to the boiler that grows narrower towards the top, and of kettle to that which grows wider', but he adds that 'in authors they are confounded [confused]'. For Webster in 1828 it was 'a vessel … with a wide mouth, usually without a cover'. The reference to 'a kettle singing on the fire' in 1866 (*OED*) should indicate the lid and narrow spout necessary to create the whistling, and it is probable that the adoption of the word for this design developed through the early nineteenth century.

Lounge. 'To lounge' as a verb is linked to other Germanic words for moving lazily and lying about. Wedgwood quotes *umeluntschen*, 'to lie about without sleeping', and Bavarian *lunzeln*, 'to doze', as well as the Swiss adjective *lündsch*, meaning 'soft and pliable'. Bailey a century earlier linked it to the Dutch *lunderen*, 'to idle or live lazily'. In Middle French there was the word *longis*, meaning a 'slow or lazy person', mainly derived from the Latin *longus*, meaning 'long'; but many etymologists make a connection to the story of Longinus, the soldier who speared Christ's body at the Crucifixion, and who developed into Lungis, a long and clumsy character in medieval English drama. In 1881 'lounge' was recorded as an alternative name for 'drawing-room', having been previously used for an 'arranged period of lounging'. 'To lounge' appeared in the early sixteenth century but became common only in the seventeenth century, when it was often spelt 'loundge'. During the sixteenth and seventeenth centuries some words now finishing *-nge* were spelt *-ndge*, e.g. 'spondge', 'randge' and 'hindge'.

Mattress. The thirteenth-century Middle English word *materas* came from the French word with the same spelling, deriving possibly via a number of routes from Arabic. One of these may have been via Catalan *almatrach*, itself from the Spanish *almadraque*, acquired during the period of divided control of the Iberian peninsula. The root Arabic word is the verb *taraha*, meaning 'to throw'; from this developed *al-matrah*, meaning a 'place where something is thrown', which became applied to a 'mat or cushion'. The English spelling *materasz* is recorded from 1290, with the established spelling settled during the seventeenth century. Until around 1700 the word was used to describe a 'floor covering or a protective cover for plants'.

Pillow. The Old English word for 'pillow' was *pyle*, which developed into the Middle English *pilwe*. This is derived from the Medieval Latin *pulvinus* and the earlier Latin *puluinus*, meaning 'cushion or pillow', which was adopted by many Germanic languages, such as Old Saxon (*puli*), and Old High German (*pfuluwi*, with variations). The double *l* in the middle of the words appeared during the fifteenth century, with the final *e* persisting into the seventeenth century. Johnson gives the word *pillowbeer* as 'the case for a pillow'.

Wall. Johnson provided a list of derivations for 'wall', including Welsh *wal*, Latin *vallum*, Old English *pall* and Dutch *walle*; the Old English *pal* may have derived from the Latin *palus*, 'a stake', and ultimately developed into 'paling' and 'palisade', but was not part of the etymology of 'wall'. One later proposal is that the Latin *vallum*, 'palisade', had been acquired by Germanic speakers before the first period of migration in the fifth century, and that the possible trace of the word in Latin-influenced Celtic helped its early establishment in Old English as *weall* or *weal*. The spelling 'wall' appeared very early, but in the sixteenth century the variants 'vall', 'waule' and 'wawle' appeared. The saying 'to go to the wall', dating from the sixteenth century, derives from the proverb 'the weakest goes to the wall', and a newer phrase not only modifies this but appears to mean completely the opposite: 'to go to the wall for someone' means 'to spare no effort to support or save someone'.

Law

Above-board. Johnson clearly defined this as coming from card-playing, 'borrowed from gamesters, who, when they put their hands under the table, are changing their cards'. The expression had been in use since the early seventeenth century. The use of the word 'board' for 'table' dates back to the late period of Old English but its use mostly disappeared during the period of Middle English. During the 1920s 'boards' was a slang word for 'playing-cards'.

Accomplice. At the beginning of the eighteenth century an 'accomplice' was a 'complice', literally someone who was 'complicit' in an affair; during the century both forms came into use, so that Johnson's *Dictionary* in 1790 has 'complice' and 'accomplice'. The word is related to 'complex' and 'complicate', as well as 'pliers', in the sense of things being brought together, the Latin root being *plicare*, meaning 'to fold', which translated to *ploier* in Old French.

Burgle. Surprisingly, there were 'burglars' before anyone 'burgled', the verb not being recorded before the nineteenth century, and then as a novelty; but 'burglar' appears in the fifteenth century, and 'burglary' in the sixteenth. The root word *burg*, meaning 'fortified settlement', is the source for this word, since burglars are associated with thefts from houses in built-up areas. Blackstone's *Commentaries on the Laws of England* (1768) states that burglary cannot be committed 'in a tent or a booth erected at a market or fair' (*OED*).

By-law. There are about six hundred places in England with names like Rugby, Derby and Whitby, almost all in places that were occupied by the Danes, for the word *by* means 'town or farm' in Old Norse.

A 'by-law' thus is a 'law specific to one town or settlement', rather than one of minor importance. However, this clarification is not as simple as it looks, since the first recorded use of the word is in a Latin text in 1283 (*OED*), using the spelling *bilage*, obviously heavily influenced by the Norse *bylage*. But the document was written in Kent, not an area affected by Danish settlement. By the fourteenth century the word was in wide use across the country, and in the sixteenth century the sound of the word made it appropriate to be adopted to apply to extra and subsidiary laws that were 'by' the main laws, in the same sense that a 'bypass' runs beside the main route.

Curfew. The earliest uses of the word 'curfew' refer to the ringing of a public evening bell, but the spellings of the word show that it was designed to tell citizens to put out their fires, probably as a safety measure to prevent houses catching light from fires untended at night. From this the word came to mean other kinds of night-time restriction. The Middle English spelling, *coeverfu*, which was restored in a seventeenth-century attempt at spelling reform as 'couvrefeu', shows the meaning to have been 'cover the fire'.

Gaol. Explaining English spellings can be difficult at times, and 'gaol' is one of the most difficult; Webster dismissed it as 'improperly written' – it should be 'jail', which is an alternative now more associated with American spelling. For Johnson, 'it is always pronounced and too often written "jail", and sometimes "goal"'. Skinner linked the word 'gaol' to the Spanish *jaul* or *xaula*, meaning 'hollow space', while for Bailey it came from the Old French *gayol* but was also linked to Welsh *geol*. The word was adopted into English twice, firstly from Old Norman French *gaiole* or *gaole* into Middle English as *gayhole*, then *gayole*, then *gail, gaole* and *gaol*; and secondly from Parisian French *jaiole* or *geole*, as *jaiole* or *jayle*. The *OED* proposes that the retention of the spelling 'gaol' may be 'due to statutory and official tradition', but it may now be as much a reaction to the rejection of that spelling by American English. For no explained reason the *OED* places 'jail' before 'gaol' in its entry and uses 'jail' throughout.

Judgement, judgment. It was not until the seventeenth century, by which time the word had been in use in English for three hundred years, that there appeared a spelling of this word without the letter *e* in the middle. One of the most notorious variant spellings in English, both versions, with and without the *e*, have been offered by the *OED* since its first publication. In 1828 Webster omitted the *e*, the form that has been retained fairly consistently in American English; in Britain Johnson's 1755 *Dictionary* and Barclay's 1812 *Dictionary* both omit the *e*, as does *Chambers Dictionary* in 1901. But the 1611 Authorised Version of the Bible used both spellings, 'iudgement' in Deuteronomy, and 'iudgment' in Job. It is now supposed that British usage prefers the form with *e*, but this is inconsistent. Eric Partridge in *Usage and Abusage* says that, while the form without *e* has become more common in Britain, 'most scholars have, since about 1920, recommended *judgement* as the more sensible and also as the more practical form'.

Loot. This comes from a Hindi word *lut*, which in turn can be traced back to Sanskrit *lotra*, from the root word *lup* meaning 'rob or plunder'. It is in effect military slang, which came to English via British soldiers and sailors in India. It is first recorded in 1788 in Stockdale's *Indian Vocabulary*. During the nineteenth century it made the transition from slang to being suitable for use in government documents.

Police. A variety of ideas surrounding public order and the administration and legislation of a city are contained within the Middle French word *police*, which entered Middle English in the fifteenth century and was more or less the same as 'policy'. The idea of 'maintaining civil order' is apparent in the use of 'to police' as a verb, in 1631, and the use of the word for an aspect of civic regulation and order grew through the eighteenth century. It was not until the end of the eighteenth century that the phrase 'the police' was used, at first to describe the force set up to protect shipping on the Thames, though the phrase 'a police man' was used ten years before this.

Prison. This word was adopted twice from French, first as *prisun* or *prisoun*, in the eleventh century from Norman French, and then in the fifteenth century as 'prison', from Parisian French. In the first case it would have been part of the language brought over by the

Normans, but in the second instance as a more stylish foreign word. In some cases repeat adoptions like this gave rise to different meanings (see **cattle**), sometimes, as in this case, the meaning was the same (see **gaol**). Early on, the word was used to  describe both a place and a state of imprisonment. The established spelling is recorded from the mid-sixteenth century.

Scapegoat. The vocabulary of the Authorised Version of the Bible (1611) is surprisingly small, considerably less than that used by Shakespeare, and many of the words we associate with the language of the King James Bible were not new at all. 'Scapegoat' was first used by William Tyndale in his illegal translation of the Bible made in 1530 and appears to have been a mistranslation. The phrase in Leviticus describes two goats driven into the wilderness, one for God, and the other for Azazel, which according to the Talmud was a cliff over which a goat would be driven for atonement of the people's sins as part of Yom Kippur. Tyndale read *Azazel* as two words, *ez ozel*, and translated the entire phrase as 'the goat that departs', and in order to make sense of this it was read as 'the goat that escapes', or 'the escape-goat'. But the clear narrative of the story has prevailed, rendering the meaning of 'scapegoat' as the goat that gets punished, rather than the one that gets away.

Trespass. The Anglo-Norman word *trespass* meant 'crossing over or moving across' from legality to illegality, literally 'to pass across' or 'transgress', and has been applied as a legal expression since medieval English law in the early fourteenth century. Following Wycliffe, who in his 1382 translation of the Bible used 'trespasses' as synonymous with 'sins', Tyndale used the word in his 1530 translation, though with two variant spellings in the same verse, 'treaspases' (for modern 'trespasses') and 'trespacers' (for modern 'trespassers'). Subsequently it was used in the Lord's Prayer in the Book of Common Prayer in 1549, but in the 1611 King James Bible the words 'debts' and 'debtors' are substituted.

Learning

Algebra. Algebra was the Arabic word *al-jabr*, meaning 'reunion of broken parts', sometimes applied to the process of bone-setting; the full Arabic phrase *al-jabr w-al-muqubalah* meant 'reduction and comparison by equations' (Partridge), also translated as the 'science of re-integration and equation' (*OED*), which in the early thirteenth century came into Italian or Medieval Latin in two forms: *algebra* and *almucabala*. The first English appearance of 'algebra' in 1541 was in the sense of bone-setting, with the arithmetical application being first used ten years later. Early dictionary writers proposed that the name came from the Arabic chemist Al Geber. Until the mid-seventeenth century the pronunciation was with the stress on the second syllable.

Archaeology. When Johnson included 'archaiology' in his *Dictionary* the subject was more of a pursuit for gentlemen collectors than a scientific discipline. The growth of the study during the nineteenth century gave rise to several words to describe its practitioners: 'archaiologers', 'archæologians', 'archeologues' and 'archæologs'. 'Archaiology' appeared in 1607, constructed from Greek words meaning 'ancient' and 'study'. Webster, in 1828, spelled it 'archeology', while in the 1901 edition of *Chambers Dictionary* it appears as 'archæology'.

Average. In his *Dictionary* in 1755 Johnson offered the definition 'a medium, a mean proportion'. This appears to have been a usage which derived from the equitable calculation among owners of the losses by damage accruing to goods in transit, which itself was connected to taxes imposed on goods being transported or imported, particularly by sea. Several languages in use around the Mediterranean had similar words, and these were copied in northern European languages. Other proposed links include 'the team of horses or oxen used to carry out the presumably non-standardised feudal duty of ploughing on manorial land', which appears in the Domesday Book as *avera*; and Skeat suggests the Arabic word *avar*, meaning 'damage', but with the proviso that 'the relationship … is obscure'.

Book. The ways by which the Old English *boc* or *bece*, meaning 'beech tree' became *boc*, 'charter', are as uncertain as the ways in which writing on any part of a beech tree became the word for 'book' (Johnson proposed that the 'rind' of a tree was used). Though there is general agreement that a lost Germanic form *bok-s*, meaning 'writing tablet', was related to the word for 'beech tree', the ways this developed differed among the Germanic languages. The *OED* offers the Old English *boc*, meaning 'charter', in which the idea of plural tablets or sheets became a singular collection, i.e. a 'book'. The Latin word *codex*, meaning 'block of wood', was selected in the late sixteenth century to differentiate a 'spine-hinged book' from a 'scroll' and may indicate the persistence of some underlying link between wood and books. The word *boc* was used in this way in the late ninth century, and the current spelling appeared in the fourteenth century.

Desk. The Classical Latin *discus* meant 'discus' or rarely the 'disc of a sundial'. In Late Latin this came to be *desca*, meaning 'table', which was adopted into Middle English as *deske*, the word having come directly from Latin and not through French. Though 'desk' is not immediately connected with 'dish' or 'dais', all three are derivations from the same Latin word.

Education. 'Education' had an early use that was more to do with physical care than academic training, but this fell out of use in the seventeenth century, though for a long time the word incorporated 'training in manners and the behaviour appropriate to a particular station in society'. Thomas Elyot in 1531 wrote about the 'education of them that … may be deemed worthy to be governours of the publike weale', this being the first known use of the word. The usage specifically to do with what a tutor might provide developed in the early seventeenth century, and Johnson listed the definitions as 'to breed; to bring up; to instruct youth'. The memorable statement that 'education is more to do with drawing out than putting in' refers directly to the Latin root words *ex* and *ducere*, meaning 'to lead out'.

Essay. Francis Bacon's first book, published in 1597, was called *Essays* and was probably modelled on Montaigne's book of *Essais*, published in 1580. Though both Bacon's and Montaigne's 'essays' are models of prose-writing, the word 'essay' was mostly used to describe an unfinished, speculative work. For Johnson, an 'essay' was 'a loose sally of the mind; an irregular indigested piece; not a regular and orderly composition'. Towards the end of the eighteenth century the 'essay' was more favourably regarded, though Webster did not include the word as a noun in his 1828 *Dictionary*. For him it was a verb, meaning 'to try or to test', especially in the sense of testing the purity of metals. In this the link to 'assay' is evident, and both words derive from the Old French *essai* and *assai*, from the Latin *exagere* or *exigere*, meaning 'to try, weigh, measure or examine'.

Museum. The Greek *museion* was a 'temple to the Muses', also used in antiquity as a treasure-store that could be borrowed from by the state in times of trouble. This kind of institution developed into a centre of learning and was transcribed in Latin as *museum*, the word adopted in the seventeenth century for 'Mr Ashmole's Museum at Oxford', a large part of which had been the collection of curiosities and specimens made by the Tradescants, father and son, known as Tradescant's Ark. The first recorded use of 'museum' is earlier, in 1615, describing the university at Alexandria, and the meaning changed

during the course of the century from a 'place of study' to a 'collection of objects and the building housing it'. In the seventeenth and eighteenth centuries 'museum' was often spelt 'musæum'.

Pedant. This is a word whose invention is often credited to Shakespeare, though the *OED* quotes three other well-known Elizabethan writers who used it before him. The word appears to be connected to 'pedagogy' and is connected to teaching, though its first use carried the idea of 'over-enthusiasm for exactness and following the rules'. Johnson gives 'schoolmaster' as the first definition, followed mysteriously by 'a man vain of low knowledge'. There is a possibility that the word developed as an abbreviation of 'pedagogant', literally 'being a school-teacher', or someone who never stops being one.

School. A 'school' was originally associated with leisure rather than work, coming from the Greek word *skhole*, meaning 'free time'; the idea of this time being used for profitable intellectual discussion brought about the change of meaning. The word was adopted into Latin as *schola* and was brought by missionaries to England as part of the conversion of the country to Christianity after AD 597, appearing in Old English as *skol, scol* and *scolu*. This developed into Middle English *scole;* 'schoole' was the favoured spelling in the sixteenth century, with the form 'school' being established in the eighteenth century.

Theory. Early uses of 'theory' were mostly in contexts to do with the Church, deriving from the meaning of the Greek word as 'sight or contemplation', which gave the sense of 'seeing inwardly as a result of contemplation'. The third edition of Cawdrey's *Table Alphabeticall*, in 1613, defined 'theorie' as 'the contemplation, or inward knowledge of any art'. This developed into the sense of a 'mental plan of something to be realised', and by the mid-seventeenth century a 'mental scheme that would explain phenomena'. Webster gave a clear differentiation between 'theory' and 'practice', but also between 'theory' and 'hypothesis', 'theory' being derived from inferences drawn from empirical evidence, while 'hypothesis' was an unproven proposition providing an explanation of phenomena.

Military

Admiral. Samuel Johnson confessed to being unsure of the derivation of this word, which comes ultimately from an Arabic word for 'high captain', *amir a ali* (or *a ala*), possibly through contact via conflict in the Mediterranean arena. There were many changes as the word emerged in Old French *amiré, amirant* or *almiral*; Old Spanish *almiralle*; Italian *ammiraglio*. It arrived in Middle English as *amyrayl, amyrall, ameraunt* and other variations, along the way picking up the letter *d* by association with the word 'admirable', and becoming 'admirail'. Caxton in 1480, in one of the earliest books to be printed in England, has it as 'admyral'.

Ambush. Skinner's definition of 'ambush' as 'to hide in the woods' may give the wrong impression but is etymologically accurate. The Late Latin conjectural *enboscare*, meaning 'to place in woods or bushes', from *boscus*, meaning 'wood', developed into the Italian *imboscare* and the Old French *embuscher*, which came to Middle English as *enbusse* and *inbuche*; the word developed into *enbusche*, then to *embusshe, embush*, and finally 'ambush' in the seventeenth century. In the seventeenth century there developed variant forms, 'imbosque' and 'imbosk', with the meaning of 'to hide in the woods', either for protection or to lie in wait.

Battle. Nothing illustrates the outcome of the Battle of Hastings as well as its name, 'battle' being from the Old French *bataille*, and ultimately from the Latin *battualia,* meaning 'military exercises'; it is linked to the word 'battery', to do with hitting, either in person or by gun. During the sixteenth century the spelling changed from 'bataille' to 'battel', and in the following century to 'battle'. A seventeenth century text on the life of Tamberlane shows how the word was used to mean 'troops formed up for battle': 'he divided his army into three main battels.' If Harold had won in 1066 we would probably refer to the event as the Fight of Hastings.

Gun. 'Gun' puzzled etymologists for a long time. Skeat proposed that it came from a Celtic word for 'bowl', *gwn*, and that it developed from the bowl of a catapult, but Wedgwood pointed out that the word 'gun' was never used for a catapult-type mechanism; he had 'little hesitation' in claiming it came from the French word *guigner*, 'to wink', based on the action of the gunner taking aim. Skinner gave the Latin word *canna,* 'cane', as the ultimate derivation, while Bailey and Johnson also suggested the French words *magnon* and *mangonel*, kinds of siege-engines, as possible sources, and the Icelandic word *gun*, meaning 'battle'. But Johnson pointed out that the word had appeared at a time when there was minimal contact between Britain and Iceland (though Icelanders did occasionally come to work as servants in medieval London).

The word first appeared in the fourteenth century as *gunne* and has no obvious link with any similar word for a similar item in any other European language. However, the munitions accounts for Windsor Castle in 1330 report a 'ballista' (a medieval siege-engine which hurled large stones) with the form of a horn (*de cornu*), called *Domina Gunnilda*, Gunnilda being a Scandinavian female name. It is now generally accepted that 'gun' was a diminutive of Gunnilda. Documentation exists for female names being conferred on large guns from Mons Meg to Big Bertha to Dora, Hitler's supergun used in 1942. The derivation seems unlikely, but no more than several other accepted word sources.

Rifle. The Old French *rifler*, meaning 'to scrape, scratch, strip or plunder' developed into the Middle English *rifil* or *ryfel*, meaning 'to pillage, or go through someone's clothes or possessions', before it acquired the more refined sense of 'making spiral grooves in the barrel of a gun', first documented from 1635 (*OED*). Variations of the word in its second meaning appear in many northern European languages, yet it was 1770 before a gun prepared in this way was called a 'rifle', the first documented use being in George Washington's diary.

Sergeant. The Latin word *serviens* meaning 'serving' and thus 'servant' became the Old French *sergent* or *serjant*, and this word was adopted by other Romance languages such as Italian, Spanish and Portuguese. The development of the word in Middle English can be seen from 1290, as *seriaunz*, meaning 'soldiers serving a knight', and as *sergaunz*, 'common foot-soldiers'. Around the same time, during the fourteenth century, the letter *g* began to be established in the middle of the word when used to mean a 'servant of a law court', especially a person with the job of arresting miscreants. The current distinction in spelling so that the *j* variant is applied only to the legal profession evolved during the nineteenth century.

Shrapnel. Legend states that when General Henry Shrapnel died in 1842 his family wished to commemorate him, but, being unable to afford a statue, asked that his invention should be named after him. In fact the shell that he invented in 1784 as 'spherical case shot' had been called 'shrapnel' from the point of its adoption by the army in 1803. The term 'shrapnel' was officially accepted in 1852 but had been in use long before then, as 'Shrapnel shells', 'Shrapnel's shot' and 'Shrapnel case shot'. Shrapnel himself received a pension of £1,200 for his services.

Squadron. One of the few words to suffer a typographical mistake in the first edition of Johnson's *Dictionary* (it is shown as 'squaddron', though all derivatives and quotations have a single *d*), this word clearly shows the development of a word from Latin through to Modern English. Defined by Worcester as a 'body of troops drawn up in a square', the word comes from the Latin *quadratus*, meaning 'square'. This became the Italian *squadrone* and the French *squadron*, at which point it was adopted by English, in the mid-sixteenth century. The French word continued to change, to *esquadron* and the present *escadron*. The sense in English of 'troops drawn up in a square' became obsolete before such military formations were deployed in the nineteenth century.

Sword. The sound of the *w* in 'sword' began to disappear from the twelfth century. In all the spellings of variants of 'sword' between the tenth and the sixteenth centuries there is a *w* or a *u* after the *s*. Many, but not all, of those forms were variations on *sweord* or *swerd*, which would now be easier to pronounce; pronouncing 'sword' with the *w*, and with the vowel pronounced as in 'born', seems to present problems, which are alleviated by dropping the *w*. However, we do have fairly common words – 'swarthy' and 'sworn' – which do not cause difficulties, and the word 'greensward' retains exactly the same set of sounds.

Nature

Acorn. Jonathan Swift pointed out that the spelling of a word can tell us its origin. Mulcaster in 1582 recommended the spelling 'akecorn', which could be a combination of two Old English words, for 'oak' and 'seed'. However, this spelling may have been an attempt to make sense of the meaning of the word. Palmer later pointed out that this derivation was a common misunderstanding, and that the word is more likely to derive directly from the Old English *æcern*, which developed into the Middle English *achern*, which in turn became *akern*. This came to mean the 'fruit of any tree growing on common land', particularly those that would provide forage for pigs – oak and beech; it is related to the word 'acre', Old English for 'pasture'. The spelling 'acorn' is recorded as early as 1440.

Adder. There are two potential roots for the word 'adder': the Old English *nædre*, meaning 'snake', possibly deriving via the Gothic *nadrs* from the Latin *natrix*; and the Old English *ætter*, meaning 'poison'. There is clear documentation of the loss of the initial *n* of *nædre* in Middle English between 1300 and 1500, as 'a nadder' became 'an adder'; and the *OED* points out that there was no recorded confusion of form between *nædre* and *ætter*. Though the development of *ætter* never involved the *tt* changing to *dd* (the rare 'natterjack toad' has retained the word internally perhaps), it is possible that the sound of *ætter* may have been incorporated into the name of the only venomous reptile in the British Isles; Skinner gave both roots for the etymology of 'adder', but the general belief now is more in favour of the derivation directly from *nædre*.

Bumblebee. A 1530 quote, 'I bomme, as a bombyll bee dothe', suggests the slow bumbling flight of the bee, but the Middle English word *bombeln* meant 'to buzz or boom'. 'To bumble' in the sense of 'doing something clumsily' is a later use of the word and seems to have had no connection to 'bumblebees'. The German word for the insect is *Hummel*, suggesting a common Germanic root. Partridge thought the 'hum' in 'humblebee' was from the sound, but this seems to be have been represented equally by 'hum' and 'bum'. The more common name used to be 'humblebee', but this is recorded only from after the fourteenth century. Webster and Barclay in the earlier nineteenth century had 'humblebee' and not 'bumblebee', and Darwin used 'humblebee', but in the twentieth century the 'humblebee' seems to have more or less disappeared.

Cattle. The legal phrase 'goods and chattels' appeared in Middle English as a combination of Old English 'goods' and Old French *chattels*. The Late Latin *captale* meaning 'property or goods' came in the feudal system of Norman England to mean 'movable property', known as *catel*, and consequently 'movable and transferable livestock'; and 'cattle' retains today this sense of economic units rather than animals – tellingly there is no singular form of 'cattle'. In the legal Anglo-French of the thirteenth century *catel* was superseded by the word *chattel* (plural *chateax*), an adoption from Parisian rather than Norman French, the word being occasionally used in Middle English. Up to about 1500 the spelling for the animal was 'cattel', and it only gradually became 'cattle', the spelling that has been established since 1700. Thus 'capital', 'cattle' and 'chattels' are substantially the same word, all stemming from the idea of counting heads (Latin *capita*) of the cows you owned.

Crayfish. In trying to make sense of the Old French set of sounds *crevice* or *crevis*, the word was written down in Middle English in a wide variety of spellings; perhaps in an attempt to resolve the spelling, the second syllable came to be 'fish', though the creature is not even a vertebrate. The origin of the word may be the Old High

German *crebiz*, which is clearly linked to the word that became *krebs* in German and *crab* in English. While other spellings, such as 'crevish' and 'crevice', were in use, 'crayfish' was used from the mid-eighteenth century. In America 'crawfish' has become the established form, but Webster allowed 'cray-fish', proposing that the first syllable may have come from the Welsh *crag*, meaning 'shell'.

Dog. The origin of this word has mystified etymologists; Partridge describes it as 'of obscure origin, but probably echoic', that is copying the sound of a dog, which is plausible. The word appeared in English in the eleventh century, alongside the Old English word *hund*, and spread to other European languages, often preceded by the word 'English', indicating a specific kind of 'dog'. The first spelling of the word, from around 1050, as

docga, is the only known use before the thirteenth century, when the spelling *dog* was used.

Feather. Webster tried to get the spelling 'fether' accepted into American usage, arguing that it was 'more accordant with etymology'. It was not until the sixteenth century that the word was spelt with an *a*, at about the same time that the middle consonant changed back to *th* from *d*, the change from *th* to *d* having occurred during the fourteenth century. Partridge traces the Old English *fether* back to Latin *penna* and Greek *pteron*. The Latin word served as a root for 'pennant', as well as for a derived use for a 'feather' – as a 'pen'.

Giraffe. In Thomas Bewick's *History of the Quadrupeds* of 1790 the name 'camelopard' appears under a recognisable engraving of a giraffe, though 'giraffe' had been in use for two hundred years. 'Camelopard' was a compound word describing an animal supposedly with the shape of a camel and the spots of a leopard. The first 'giraffe' in Britain was seen in 1827, and the word 'giraffe' does not feature in the 1790 edition of Johnson's *Dictionary* (which defines 'camelopard' as 'an animal taller than an elephant, but not so thick'). As the animal would have been encountered only rarely by early English speakers, it is not surprising that various versions of its name occur, deriving from a variety of source languages, including Italian *giraffa,* Old Spanish *azorofa,* Old French *girafle* and Arabic *ziraph.* A bout of Chinese whispers in the Middle English period gave rise to the versions *gerfaunt* and *orafle.*

Gull. Related to the Welsh *gwylan,* which was Webster's preferred etymology, *gull* may have entered English from Cornish *guilan* or *gullan.* It first appears in written English in a fifteenth-century cookery book. The conjectural Celtic root is *gulb,* meaning 'point', referring to the bird's conspicuous beak; this root is still there in the Gaelic *guilb,* meaning 'beak'. 'To gull', meaning 'to fool', possibly comes from the old use of the word as meaning 'to eat hungrily and indiscriminately', but a 'gull' was also 'any young bird', which would eat what was offered. The subsequent slang use has been extant since the sixteenth century.

Insect. The definition of an 'insect' as an 'animal with six legs and three sections' gives a clue to the origin of the word. Some authorities simplify this by saying an 'insect' is 'in sections'; literally it is 'cut in three parts', deriving from the Latin *insecare,* meaning 'to cut into', which has the past participle *insectum,* meaning 'having been cut into'. This is possibly misleading, a more obvious explanation being that the thin joints between the parts of an insect's body give the impression of the animal having been cut into, especially when compared to the smooth outlines of other animals. The word was first used by early scientists at the beginning of the seventeenth century. Other connected words from the Latin *secare* are 'segment', 'sector' and even 'sickle' and 'scythe'.

Mammoth. 'Mammoth' is similar to the Russian *mammant* and an earlier version, *mammot.* These derive from a Tartar word, *mamont,* which during its passage to French, German and English was misread, the *on* becoming *ou. Mamont* comes from the Tartar word for 'the earth', *mamma* or *mama.* Supposedly, Siberian peasants were puzzled by the presence of frozen and preserved mammoths in the ground; the only explanation was that they must have burrowed

their way in. Despite the happy coincidence of a word for 'earth' being the same as a child's first word for its mother, in 1882 Skeat claimed no such Tartar word had been found. There have been several other confusions though, the *OED* quoting Strahlenberg in 1738 as saying that the name 'certainly comes from the word Behemoth', and Bell in 1763 saying 'this creature called mammon'.

Newt. The Old English *efete* was a 'lizard', which became the Middle English *evete* or *ewte*. The *OED* does not record a written documentation before 1425, by which time the *n* had transferred from the article to the word itself, giving 'newte'. However, the forms 'eft' and 'evvet' survived in various British English dialects, not restricted to spoken English, until the nineteenth century; in American English the word 'eft' is used for the intermediate post-aquatic phase of a newt's development. Webster defined 'eft' as 'a newt, an evet'; 'evet' and 'evvet' seem to have disappeared. 'Newt' was classified as a 'difficult' spelling in *The Spelling Bee Guide* published in Portsmouth in 1876.

Pearl. The Old English word for 'pearl' was *meregrota* (possibly from *mere*, meaning 'sea', and *grota*, meaning 'grit'), which survives in the name Margaret, but this was displaced by the Anglo-Norman *perle*, which developed into the Middle English *peerl* and *perell*. But where *perle* came from is still disputed. Bailey suggested the Latin *spherula*, meaning 'little ball', Serjeantson suggested the Vulgar Latin *perla*, meaning 'pearl', while Partridge suggested a Sanskrit–Greek–Latin route leading to the Latin *perna*, meaning 'mussel', which is the same form as southern Italian dialect words for 'pearl'. The form *perla* spread throughout Europe, appearing in languages as far apart as Catalan and Old Icelandic, and with derivative meanings as distinct as 'teeth' and a 'capsule for holding medicine'.

Scavenger. Any form of the word 'scavenger' looks as if it will have to do with the unpleasant but necessary business of removing the waste and leavings of life in all its forms. But ultimately this word comes from early French and Old English words to do with 'examining'. A 'scavager' (the *n* has crept in to help pronunciation – see **orchard**) was a person with the duty of 'scavage', specifically 'the inspection of goods brought into a marketplace by a travelling seller', and later collecting taxes due on such goods. From that the job developed into attending to the cleaning of streets, presumably after street markets, which gradually took over as the more important task.

The use of the word to describe the actions of animals that feed on decaying matter has been around for over five hundred years. During the Industrial Revolution a 'scavenger' was also a 'child who had to crawl about under the machinery in a spinning-mill collecting cotton waste'.

Tadpole. Tadpoles were once wonderfully called 'porwigles', 'pollywiggles' or 'pollywogs', and also 'bullheads', the last a name later transferred to a small fish. A 'tadpole' may be the young either of a frog or a toad, but the word is formed from the Old English word *tadde* or *tada,* meaning 'toad', and *poll,* meaning 'head', as in 'poll tax'. Johnson quotes Thomas Browne as saying a tadpole was 'what the ancients called a gyrinus', a Latin word meaning 'moving in coils or circles', which later became the zoological name for the genus of whirligig beetles. *Poll* also appears in 'pollard', in effect the removal of the head of the tree, or cutting it in such a way as to leave a large head.

Science

Alcohol. The first references in English to 'alcohol', occurring in the sixteenth century, are to a fine powder used as eye-shadow, now usually called 'kohl', obtained from North Africa; thus the root of the word is Arabic. The method of obtaining this substance led to the use of the word for any product of sublimation, first for powders and then, but not until around 1670, for 'pure liquid spirit'. By this stage it was being spelt 'alcahol' or 'alcool'. 'Alcohol' as the 'rectified spirit present in wine' was in use by the early eighteenth century.

Ammonia. 'Salts of ammonium' were first collected in antiquity near the Temple of Amun in Libya (or Lybia, in Bailey's 1746 *Dictionary*). The Greek form of the god's name, *Ammon*, gave rise to the name of this substance, collected either as rock or by a process of distillation of camel dung. The material, used as the active component in smelling salts, but more widely as a powerful leavening agent, later became known as 'sal volatile', 'sal ammoniac' and 'spirits of hartshorn', the last of these from the process of dry distillation from horns and hooves. The root has produced a number of words. The gas 'ammonia' was obtained from ammonium carbonate by the Swedish chemist Torbern Bergman in 1782; and the god Ammon was often portrayed as bearing ram's horns, the form of which can be seen in the word 'ammonite'. 'Sal armoniak' appears in 1386 in Chaucer, as an ingredient in alchemy.

Atmosphere. A combination of two Greek words meaning 'air' and 'sphere', this word was coined by Bishop John Wilkins in 1638, in the form 'atmosphæra', though he was in this case describing the space around the moon, now known to have a barely perceptible atmosphere. Wilkins went on to propose a universal language, in which the alphabetic construction of a word could function as a classification system. Thus (as quoted by Borges) *deba* means 'flame', from *de*, an 'element', *deb*, 'fire as the first element', *deba*, 'the first aspect of a fire'. Though not adopted, his plan influenced later constructed languages. Despite being omitted from Johnson's *Dictionary* in 1755, 'atmosphere' was taken up and remains with us.

Atom. Isidore of Seville, writing an encyclopedia in the seventh century, knew that an 'atom' was both invisible and indivisible. The word arrived in English in the sixteenth century from French as 'atome' (from Greek via Latin) and became anglicised to 'atom'. Shakespeare, in *Romeo and Juliet*, used 'atomies' to mean 'tiny fairies'. Long before this, in medieval thought, an *attome* (as spelt in 1398) already existed, as 'the smallest division of time', in a scale which included ounces and moments, and was equivalent to 'the twinkling of an eye', that is a blink.

Chemistry. For the root of this word we have to go back to the Egyptian word for 'black mud', *khmi*, which gave the people living in Egypt the name of their land, *Khamè* or *Khem*. During the Roman Empire the land of *Khemia*, as it was pronounced in Greek, was famous for the skill of transmuting base metals into gold and silver, which, during the period of contact between Arabic speakers and the Latin-based languages, became known as *al-chemia*, or *alkamy* in Middle English. This developed into 'alchemy' by the seventeenth century, by which time it was perceived mostly as fraud; however, its practitioners were by then known as 'chemists', and it was this word that came to be used for the empirical natural philosophers of the late seventeenth and eighteenth centuries. Johnson gave the word as 'chemistry or chymistry', from the Greek word *kema*, meaning 'juice or melt', from the 'Oriental' word for 'black'. 'Chymistry' was still given as the primary spelling in Barclay's dictionary in 1812.

Electricity. Johnson was clearly excited by the possibilities of 'electricity', which he defined in two forms, 'attraction caused by rubbing' and 'static electricity'; he reported the phenomenon as bearing 'a multitude of philosophical wonders'. 'Electricity' derives from *elektron*, the Greek for 'amber', which attracts fibres when rubbed. Sir Thomas Browne first used 'electric' and 'electricity' in 1646 in his book *Common Fallacies*, though William Gilbert, in his 1600 book in Latin, *De Magnete*, used the Latin form *electrum*. The concept of 'electricity' as a power to be harnessed, and the use of the word in this way, appeared in the early nineteenth century. In the seventeenth century a final *k* was often added in the spelling of 'electrick', as was the case with many words ending -*ic*.

Galaxy. A Greek myth explained the stars as drops of milk from the breast of Hera, consort of Zeus. *Gala* is Greek for 'milk'; for Isidore of Seville, this was why the Gauls were so called – *Galli* obviously meant 'people with milk-white skin'. More realistically, *gala* was the root for the Latin *lac*, and was the basis of the Greek and Latin *galaxias*, for the band of stars known also as the 'Milky Way'; Johnson defines 'galaxy' simply as 'the Milky Way'. *Galaxias* was adopted directly into English in the fourteenth century, but at the same time the form *galaxy* was used as well. Chaucer explained the word clearly: 'the Galaxye which men clepeth [call] the Milky Wey, for hit is whyt.'

Nicotine. *Nicotiane* was an early French name for the tobacco plant. Jean Nicot (1530–1600) was the French ambassador to Portugal, who around 1560 sent some tobacco seeds to the French court. The plant was named by Leonhart Fuchs (1501–66), professor of medicine at the university of Tübingen, and author in 1542 of *De historia stirpium commentarii insignes* (*Notable Commentaries on the Histories of Plants*). *Nicotiana tabacum* was included in his encyclopedia of plants, unpublished at his death. The *tabacum* section of the scientific name comes from the Carib word for the Y-shaped inhalation-tubes used by the people of Haiti and Cuba to breathe in the smoke of the burning leaves, as observed by Columbus and his fellow explorers in 1492. The active constituent 'nicotine' was isolated in the early nineteenth century in France, as *nicotaine*, which around 1820 was translated into English as 'nicotin' but later became established as 'nicotine'.

Parasite. Robert Cawdrey in 1604 defined 'parasite' as a 'base flatterer, or soothing companion'. For Johnson in 1755 it meant 'one that frequents rich tables and earns his welcome by flattery'. It was not until the eighteenth century that the word was used to describe a 'plant growing on a host'. The derivation, from Greek words for 'beside' and 'food', refers to the earlier usage of 'one who sits beside a host and eats his food'.

Robot. English has borrowed few words from Czech; *robota* is the Czech for 'forced labour' and is similar to the Russian word for 'work', *rabota*. These come from the Gothic word *arbaiths* meaning 'labour, distress, trouble', which also gave rise to the German *arbeit*, meaning 'work'; but the development of the root-words can be traced further back, through Slavic words for 'servitude' and 'slave', to words relating to inheritance and being an orphan, from the Latin *orbus*, meaning 'deprived'.

Karel Capek's play *R.U.R.* (*Rossum's Universal Robots*) was translated into English in 1923, and 'robot' was adopted into English, though the word had been used previously in a short story by Capek's brother Josef.

Scientist. *The Quarterly Review* for 1834 published the summary of a debate during which there had been an attempt to determine a generic word for those working in the various branches of science. The word 'scientist' was rejected as 'not generally palatable' (*OED*). The word was created by analogy with similar words – 'artist', 'economist', 'atheist', etc., and its acceptance is usually credited to William Whewell, who re-proposed it in 1840. Partridge proposes that there is more than a shadow of a link to Boccaccio's *scienzato* (fourteenth century), meaning 'learned man'; and the word ultimately derives from the Latin *scire*, meaning 'to know'.

Sports and Games

Athlete. The Greek word *athletes* was 'someone who contended for a prize', and it is as a description of a Greek competitor that the word was used in the sixteenth and seventeenth centuries, in its Latin form, *athleta*. For Bailey in 1721 an 'athlete' was a 'wrestler', but Johnson did not include it in his 1755 *Dictionary*, though it appeared in later editions of the work and was certainly in use by 1755; contemporary writers noted the omission. Lemon's *English Etymology* in 1783 includes 'athlete', with 'athleta' as an internal entry, but not 'athletic', while in 1828 Webster enlarged upon the physical aspects of competition in his entry for 'athletic', defining 'athlete' as 'contender for victory'. The development of athletic activities through the nineteenth century is reflected in the use of the word. Reid, in 1853, gave the definition 'a contender for victory of strength; a wrestler', while Cooley eight years later gave 'one who contends for victory in public games'.

Bridge (contract). The game 'bridge' or 'contract bridge', which was imported from Turkey and/or Russia in the late nineteenth century, has no connection with the construction spanning a river, etc. The name is said to come from the Russian form of whist, *biritch*, which means 'herald or announcer', and the game was originally also called 'Russian whist'. According to early documentation of the game, in 1886, 'biritch' was said instead of 'no trumps'.

Champion. A 'champion' is essentially a 'man in a field', for the Latin *campus* was a 'ground for military or athletic exercises', a development of the meaning 'field'. This gave rise to the Late Latin *campio*, 'combatant in the arena', and *campiones*, which Isidore of Seville defined as 'gladiators'. The word arrived in English twice, in Old English as *cempa* (Beowulf is described as a *cempa*), and then as *champiun* as an adoption from French in 1225. The sense of 'to champion' appeared in nineteenth-century medievalist writing, deriving from the role of a 'champion', who from the thirteenth century was 'one who fought as an individual on someone else's behalf'.

Chess. Chess arrived in England around the end of the first millennium, and the roots of the word can be traced back to a sixth-century Indian game called *chaturanga*, which became the Persian *chatrang* and the Arabic *shât-ranj*. The game was brought to Europe via a number of routes, the best-documented being through North Africa and Muslim Spain, providing the Spanish word *ajedrez* and the Portuguese *xadrez*. However, the Medieval Latin, Italian and French versions of the name of the game were all plural ending words, probably deriving from pluralisation of the Persian word *shah* (which may be linked to Russian *tsar* and the Latin *Caesar*). The Latin *scacci* became the Italian *scacchi*, the Provençal *escacos* and the Anglo-Norman *eschès*, leading to the Middle English 'chess' or 'chesse', in the early fourteenth century. One of the first books printed in England was Caxton's *Game and Playe of the Chesse* (1474). Variant forms 'cheast' and 'chest' appeared in the sixteenth and seventeenth centuries.

Cricket. The origin of the word has exercised scholars as much as the origin of the game, and the *OED* acknowledges that the etymology is uncertain. Skeat's proposal that the Old English *crice*, meaning 'staff', would give the diminutive form *cricet*, meaning 'little staff', sounds plausible. Wedgwood pointed to the Dutch word *kraakstool*, and the Norse *krakk*, both meaning 'three-legged stool', and Bailey proposed a derivation from the Old English *cryce*, meaning 'stick'.

Webster noted that the Old French word *criquet* meant a 'goal stake' in the game of bowls. Partridge, clearly looking at early images of the game, noted that early wickets had only two uprights and a crossbar, and thus felt there was a plausible link to the Old French *croc*, meaning 'hook'. However, none of these is fully satisfactory; Wedgwood pointed out that the word 'cricket' was never used for the bat, but neither is there evidence for it being used for the wicket (a word that has been in use since 1733). Perhaps we have to settle for improbabilities, such as the 1622 description of the game as similar to a Persian game called *Kuitskaukan* (*OED*). However, a 1648 Wenceslaus Hollar engraving shows protestors throwing at 'the Archprelate of St Andrewes' 'cricketts, stooles, sticks and stones'; a 'crickett' here appears to be a 'three-legged stool'.

Goal. Middle English *gol* developed from Old English *galan*, meaning 'to impede or stop a movement'; in this sense your 'goal' was not so much something that you aimed for, but rather what stopped you achieving it. Alternatively, Webster proposed that it came from the French *gaule*, meaning an 'end aimed at'; but this also might mean a 'starting post for a contest'. And for Bailey, it came from the Dutch *gaule* or *goel*, meaning a 'pole set in the ground to mark the point for runners in a race to make for'. Johnson was understandably confused by Dryden's 1697 use of the word for both the start and the end of a race. The *OED* marks it appropriately as 'of difficult etymology'.

Jockey. Most English words that derive from Hebrew have something to do with Jewish culture; 'jockey' is one of the exceptions. Walter Skeat proposed that ultimately this word derived from Hebrew, via Greek, Latin and then French. The Hebrew name *Ya'aqob*, meaning 'one who seizes by the heel', became the Greek and Latin *Iacobus*, and French *Jacques*, ultimately leading to 'Jack'. Just as 'Jack' became 'Jock' in Scotland, 'Jockey' was a northern pronunciation of the diminutive form. The association with horses is found early on in the history of the word, but not till the end of the seventeenth century specifically for riders in a horse-race.

Sport. In its current form 'sport' dates from the sixteenth century, and this derives from a Middle English form *disport*, from the Old French *desport*. Tulloch proposes that 'sport' is something that 'carries you away', matching the two Latin roots, *des*, meaning 'away', and *portare*, meaning 'to carry'; this sense is now more accurately conveyed by the word 'transport', except in a legal sense, where *desport* lost the letter *s* to become 'deport'. By the nineteenth century 'disport' was only to be found in archaic and poetic use; 'desport' had disappeared by 1500. The first activity documented as a sport we would recognise was 'gouff', noted in the Acts of Parliament of Scotland in 1491.

Tennis. The usual etymology for 'tennis' is a derivation from French *tenez*, an instruction to 'receive this', or 'here it comes'. The word appeared first in Middle English as *tenetz*, from which it developed into *teneys*, *tenyce*, *tenyse* and *tennice*. However, Partridge credits Webster with the idea that it came from the Egyptian city of Tinnis, where the soft fabrics were made that constituted the covers of early tennis balls. This view is supported by the derivation of 'racket' or 'racquette' from the Arabic *rahet*, meaning 'palm of the hand', since early tennis was played with this rather than a racket.

Umpire. This is one of a handful of words in which an initial *n* has transferred from the word itself to the indefinite article in front, changing *a numper* into *an umper*. In this case the shift was established well before the end of the Middle English period, the word having arrived as French *noumpere*, from *non peer*, that is 'one who can adjudicate by virtue of not being one of a pair of combatants'. The vowel sound also shifted in the same way that *frere* in Anglo-Norman became 'friar' in Middle English. The spelling 'umpire' was established in the seventeenth century. Samuel Johnson believed the word derived from *un pere*, presumably 'one who could deliver a decision with patriarchal authority'.

State and Politics

Ballot. In ancient Athens a person who incurred the wrath of the people could be banished by popular vote, citizens gathering to register his name on a fragment of pottery called an *ostrakon*, which has provided us with the word 'ostracise'. The modern 'ballot' also derives from the object used to register the vote, originally a 'small marked ball', as used in the government of the Venetian Republic. The word came into English from the Italian *ballotta*, via the French *ballotte*, at the beginning of the sixteenth century. 'To blackball' someone originally meant to give a vote against that person by choosing a black ball rather than a white one to put into a voting urn; it dates from the late nineteenth century.

Borough. The Germanic and Old Norse variations on *burh* and *burg* are generally accepted to have meant some kind of 'fortified place', and for the period of Old English a settlement with any kind of fortification would have needed the organisation and administration of materials and labour, leading to the sense of 'town or civic community'. The Old English *burgh* developed into a large number of local variants and derivatives, such as *burhwaru*, meaning 'body of men'; but the form *burrough*, which was the form most in use until early Modern English, was replaced by 'borough' in most of

Britain, except Scotland, where the form 'burgh' was preferred. 'Burrow' may be a development of the word, in its sense of 'stronghold', but this derivation is not widely accepted.

Bureaucracy. The French word *bureau*, meaning 'writing desk', is derived from *burel*, the coarse cloth used to cover the wood of a desk. The second part of 'bureaucracy' derives from *kratia*, Greek for 'rule', which appears in 'democracy', 'autocracy', etc. The adoption of the word after the Napoleonic Wars may be due to contact with French administrative systems, and it has generally been used in a pejorative way. Being not only foreign, but even combining two foreign roots, 'bureaucracy' and its derivative 'bureaucrat' have provoked anger on many fronts. Fowler wrote in 1906: 'its mongrel origin is flaunted in our faces'; and the 1983 edition of *Fowler's Modern English Usage* states: 'the formation is so irregular that all attempt [sic] at self-respect in pronunciation may as well be abandoned.'

Candidate. Candidates for office in ancient Rome dressed in white togas to symbolise their honesty and suitability for public service, so it was said; the Latin for 'white' being *candidus*, the description was also applied directly to the person. The word is recorded in the third edition of Cawdrey's dictionary (1613) and would have been considered by some as an inkhorn term. 'Candid', meaning 'open, without deceit', is a clear development of the meaning.

Economy. 'Economy' arrived in English in the fifteenth century from the Middle French *yconomie* and *economie*, meaning 'management of a household', to develop suddenly with a wide variety of spellings and meanings. The spellings within the first hundred years include *iconomy, yconomy, yconomye, iconimie, iconomie, iconomye, oeconomye, yconomi* and *yconomie* (*OED*), while the meanings developed to include 'the good use to which something may be put', 'good administrative order', 'restraint in expenditure' and 'the harmonious arrangement of parts within a whole'. A general sense of 'probity in administration' overshadows these, echoing the Late Latin usages for 'arrangement, administration and organising'. These developed from the Greek word *oekonomia* for the (generally thrifty) 'management of a household' (an *oekonomus* was a 'house-steward').

Before the application to financial matters, which developed in the late nineteenth century, there was a wide range of applications, biological, theological and aesthetic. The sense of frugality developed in the late seventeenth century, around the time the spelling was established as 'oeconomy'; the current spelling dates from the nineteenth century.

Mandarin. This word, with its connotations of inscrutable Chinese regional governors or discreet and powerful senior civil servants, does not derive from China at all. Its first documented use in English, in 1589, shows it in use in Portuguese settlements in India as *mandarim*; it arrived through Hindi or Malay from the Sanskrit word *mantrin* meaning 'counsellor'. Variations of the spelling included 'mandeline' and 'mandorin'. The use of the word for the small orange-like fruit, which did originally come from China, dates from 1820.

Mint. 'Mint', as a place where coins are made, was a word adopted by Germanic languages from Latin before the period of first migration in the fifth century. The word appears as *mynet*, meaning 'coin', with connected words *mynetian*, meaning 'to mint or coin', and *mynetere*, meaning 'money-changer'. Perhaps the phrase 'to make a mint' carries a more literal meaning than might at first appear. The Latin root was *moneta*, meaning 'coins or a mint'. By the sixteenth century the spelling was changing to 'mynt', which became established as 'mint' by about 1650. The predominant use of the word for a 'place of making coins' was established by about 1650.

Mob. Early eighteenth-century writers who were against the use of abbreviations in English complained about how the the Latin phrase *mobile vulgus*, meaning 'the easily swayed crowd', was being shortened to 'mob'. Swift observed its use even in church sermons (he also complained about the use of 'sham', 'bubble' and 'bully'). By then its use was not limited to 'a rioutous assembly', and poets such as Pope were using the word satirically to make fun of any group of people. Webster in 1806 gave the word not as a noun, but only as a verb, meaning 'to scold, harrass, riot, overbear, press'. The association with a sense of movement has been retained, and not just in a derogatory sense: in nineteenth-century Australia the word came to be applied to a group of workmen got together for a job, such as a 'mob of shearers' (*OED*).

Palace. The Palatine Hill in Rome was the location of the residence of the Emperor Augustus and thus gave its name to the Late Latin word *palatium*, meaning 'royal residence'. The hill was possibly once fortified with stakes, the Latin *palus*, meaning 'stake', giving the ultimate root for the word 'palatine', meaning 'having royal privileges'. The word *palatium* gradually lost status till by the  twelfth century it came to mean 'town hall'. While 'palace', which entered Middle English in the fourteenth century, has been applied to the most important residences, the twentieth-century re-adoption of the French form *palais,* for 'dance-hall', brought the environment of quasi-regal glamour to the less privileged.

Prime minister. The earliest uses of this term, in the late seventeenth century, were unofficial and merely descriptive and came to have overtones of distaste with connotations of despotism. Robert Walpole was *de facto* Prime Minister from 1721 to 1742 but disowned the term, as his post as First Lord of the Treasury placed him at the head of the administration anyway. The terms 'premier' and 'first minister' were preferred during the eighteenth century, and official usage began in the 1870s, with full use of the term for the head of the administration being royally acknowledged in 1905.

Prime comes from the Latin *primus*, meaning 'first', and 'minister' ultimately comes from the Latin *minor*, meaning 'less', for one person who assists another (the opposite of *magister*, from *magis*, meaning 'more', from which we get 'magistrate').

Pundit. The Hindi word *pandit* comes from the Sanskrit *pandita*, defined by the *Hobson-Jobson Dictionary* as 'properly a man learned in Sanskrit lore', i.e. Indian philosophy. As the word was adopted into English it became applied to specific roles within the British Raj: the 'Pundit of the Supreme Court' was a local adviser to the British judges on matters of Hindu law. By 1850 it was being applied to Indian people trained by the British to survey areas beyond the frontiers of British India. This application arose from the first two people employed in this way, who were school-teachers – 'pundit' being effectively the equivalent of 'Sir' or 'Miss'.

The word is recorded from the sixteenth century in French, Spanish and Portuguese as well as English, transcribed as 'pandit', 'pendet', 'pandite', 'pandect' and 'pandecta'; according to *Hobson-Jobson* 'pandit' may have been nearer the indigenous pronunciation for a large part of India. The first spelling as 'pundit' appeared in 1698, but this did not become established until the late eighteenth century. The transfer into English use as 'an expert in any field' appeared as early as 1816.

Regime. Does the disappearance of an accent over a vowel in a foreign word in common use signify its wholehearted acceptance into English? After 'regime' was introduced in the late eighteenth century, it was used for a long time without an accent over the *e*, this reappearing in the early twentieth century. Around this time it was criticised by Fowler in *The King's English* as 'an unnecessary French word', to be rejected in favour of 'administration' (which had of course arrived from France during the Middle English period). Partridge, in *Usage and Abusage*, states clearly that without the accent it is an English word; in italicised format and 'so treated as a French word, it must bear an accent'.

Socialism. For Joseph Worcester in his 1860 *Dictionary* 'socialism' was a general term covering a variety of 'schemes of social arrangement involving abandonment or modification of one or more of a list of principles including private property, individual industry and enterprise, and the right of marriage and the family'. A rather different view appears in the 1972 *Chambers Twentieth Century Dictionary*, where it is defined as a 'theory, principle or scheme of social organisation which places the means of production and distribution in the hands of the community'. The root word is the Latin *socius*, meaning 'companion'; 'socialism' was first used in the 1830s, there being some dispute as to whether it originated in France or England.

Tools and Materials

Anvil. Skinner in 1671 noted that the Old English form *ænfilt* was similar to other Germanic words for 'anvil', which may have come from the Latin for 'anvil', *incus*, deriving from *in* and *cudere*, meaning 'to strike on'. Various spellings occur in the period of transition from Old to Middle English: *onfilti, anfilt, anfilte*, before fourteenth-century versions *anuelt, anuylt* and *anduell*. The letter *d* after *n* seems to have appeared in the fourteenth century and dropped away after about a hundred years. The King James Bible of 1611 has 'anuill', but up to the eighteenth century *u* and *v* were treated as vowel and consonant forms of the same letter.

Axe. The Old English *æx* survived the introduction of the French word *gisarme*, which appears in the second half of Layamon's poem *Brut*, written in the thirteenth century. The word had been brought to England as *auks* by migrants from the Continent, where European languages ranging from Swedish to Gothic developed variants from the Greek *axine*, meaning 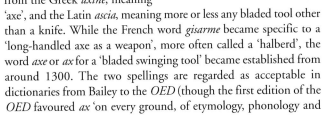 'axe', and the Latin *ascia*, meaning more or less any bladed tool other than a knife. While the French word *gisarme* became specific to a 'long-handled axe as a weapon', more often called a 'halberd', the word *axe* or *ax* for a 'bladed swinging tool' became established from around 1300. The two spellings are regarded as acceptable in dictionaries from Bailey to the *OED* (though the first edition of the *OED* favoured *ax* 'on every ground, of etymology, phonology and analogy'), but Webster directed that the spelling should be 'ax' and that the spelling 'axe' was 'improperly written'.

Bulldozer. 'To bulldoze' someone was a term used in America for intimidatory violence by whites on blacks, first used around 1880; a 'bulldoze' was a 'bull-dose', a dose of violence supposedly large enough to calm a bull. Probably the lightness of tongue required for the pronunciation of 'bulldosed' led to the change of spelling to 'bulldoze', with its meaning of 'powering your way to get what you want'. The extension to the earth-moving vehicle retains the idea of threat, with the idea of the machine used as an aggressively destructive force.

Knife. 'Knife' was adopted from Old Norse quite late on in the period of contact with the Scandinavians, in the eleventh or twelfth century. Old Norse *knifr* became Old English *cnif,* replacing the word *seax,* which it has been proposed had given the Saxons their name. The sound of *k* at the beginning of the word was dropped during the seventeenth century, while the spelling change from *c* to *k* took place during the thirteenth century. The plural spelling *knives* was established during the seventeenth century. Webster tried to change the accepted American spelling to 'nife' and 'nives', but with this and other words beginning *kn-* he was unsuccessful.

Marble. The thirteenth-century poem called *Brut,* about the early history of Britain, has survived in two parts written with fifty years between them; over this period the word for 'marble' changed from *marmon-stane* to *marbre.* Both these forms came from the Old French *marbre,* from the Latin word *marmor. Marbre* developed into 'marbel', and later the form we have today. The Latin comes from the Greek *marmaros,* from the word *marmarein,* meaning to sparkle, referring to the tiny reflecting facets in the unpolished stone. The *OED* gives 1681 for the first use of 'marbles' to describe the small hard balls of glass, remarkably late given the evidence for the antiquity of the game.

Metal. The Latin word *metallum* means 'mine or quarry' and comes from the Greek *metallon,* meaning 'mine', which itself comes from the word *metallan,* meaning 'to go in search of'. Metal is thus essentially 'something not to hand', but 'a material that has to be searched for'; the Greek prefix *meta-* can carry the meaning of 'quest or pursuit'. The word was adopted into Middle English from French in the thirteenth century; it seems that Old English did not class the various 'metals' into a single grouping. Early forms of the word were *mettall* and *metall*, but the established spelling was arrived at by the mid-eighteenth century.

Porcelain. Johnson thought that this word was derived from the French *pour cent années* referring to the European belief that in China the materials of 'porcelain' were matured underground for a hundred years. The real derivation is equally bizarre: the first 'porcelain' to arrive in the West from China would have passed along the Silk Road and entered Europe via Italy, where its resemblance to the Venus shell, known as *porcella*, gave it the name *porcellana*. The shell in turn had received its name as a diminutive of *porca* from its resemblance to part of a sow's anatomy. In Cockeram's 1670 *Dictionarie* it was spelt 'porcelane', with the definition 'China dishes'.

Scissors. During the sixteenth century attempts to rationalise English spelling to make sense of the forms of words largely involved reshaping spellings to show links to Latin and Greek, sometimes invented. Thus the Middle English word *sisoures*, which had indeed come via Old French *cisoires* from a Latin word *caedere*, meaning 'to cut', was reshaped to include a *c* as a reference to another Latin word, *scindere*, which also meant 'to cut'. The two forms, with and without the letter *c*, survived side by side for over a hundred years, from 'scissoures' and 'siszers' (1568 and 1580 respectively) to 'scissers' and 'sizzers' (1673 and 1719 respectively). Small wonder that Johnson in 1755 felt unable to offer a definitive spelling or etymology: 'cisors' from *caedere*; 'scissors' from *scindere*; 'cisars, cizars, or scissars' from the French *ciseaux*.

Sledgehammer. The Old English word *slean*, meaning 'to strike an object', was the root for *slecg*, 'hammer'. The Old English word *hamor* came from a Scandinavian root suggesting a stone weapon rather than a tool; so *slecg* was perhaps more of a tool than a weapon. Wedgwood proposes that the word imitates the sound of hitting with a large hammer. 'Sledge', defined by Reid in 1853 as 'large heavy hammer', became specific to a larger industrial-type tool, and perhaps the word 'hammer' was added to make its use clear to the layperson. The other kind of 'sledge' comes from Dutch, from a culture long accustomed to travelling on frozen surfaces, and is related to 'slide'.

Spade. The 'spades' which appear in a deck of playing-cards derive from the Spanish and Portuguese *espada*, though as this design transferred to first French and then British playing-cards it came to look more like a digging tool than a sword. Words similar to 'spade' meaning 'digging tool' are common to several Germanic languages, from Icelandic to Dutch, and may derive from the Greek *spathe*, meaning 'blade of a paddle or sword'. In the *Corpus Glossary*, an eighth-century glossary of Latin and Old English words, the Latin *vangas* is translated as *spadan*. The anonymous author may claim to be the first person who called a spade a spade.

Umbrella. Literally 'little shade', this word arrived from Italian in the seventeenth century. Cockeram in 1670 defined an umbrella as a 'screen wherewith men cover themselves from the sun'. It seems that until the mid-eighteenth century there was an English word for something to protect yourself from the sun, but not from rain. In 1832 Webster's *Dictionary* included the variant 'umbrel' and pointed out that it could be used against rain or snow. Johnson pragmatically stated that an umbrella could be used 'in hot countries to keep off the sun, and in others to bear off the rain'.

Trade and Money

Coin. 'Coin' can be traced through the Old French *coing*, meaning 'corner' or 'wedge', to the Latin *cuneus* meaning 'corner', the root being the wedge-shaped die used to strike a 'coin'. This would link with the wedge-shaped stone and many wedge-shaped tools used in letterpress, gunnery and stowage all known as a 'quoin'. The first use of 'coin' as 'money' appears in Chaucer's *Troilus and Criseyde*, in the late fourteenth century. The Middle English *coyne* or *coyn* became 'coin' by about 1600, with the words 'to coin a phrase' being first recorded in 1589.

Debt. During the sixteenth century increasing scholarship led to a new appreciation of Latin, and the desire to bring out the Latin basis of common words can be seen in the spelling 'dettes' in a version of the Lord's Prayer in 1400, giving way to 'debtes' in a 1557 version. The Latin base is *debere*, meaning 'to owe', which developed into later spoken Latin *pecunia debita,* meaning 'money owed', which became Old French *dette.* The sense of a 'duty' or a 'favour or task owing to someone else' developed as the word was adopted into English, though these uses are now declining: Barclay's 1812 *Dictionary* gives the meaning 'that which any man is obliged to do or suffer'. A few figurative or symbolic uses, such as the phrase 'a debt of honour', have survived, but many, such as 'the debt to nature', a poetic euphemism for death, have disappeared.

Dollar. Partridge gives a very exact origin for the word 'dollar': 'a coin worth 3 marks, short for *Joachimsthaler*, made, 1519 onwards, at Joachimst(h)al, St Joachim's Valley, in Bohemia'. This story is given also in Worcester's *Dictionary* of 1862, but with the alternative derivations of the Old English *dæl*, meaning 'portion, being a part or portion of a ducat', or the Swedish *daler*, 'from the town of Dale or Daleburg where it was coined'. By 1600 it had become 'dollar' in English, and the 'Spanish dollar' was in wide use as a monetary unit in America before its official adoption in the United States in 1785.

Expensive. The introduction of new words into the language during the sixteenth century provoked strong reactions; it is hard to imagine that an apparently indispensable word such as 'expensive' should have been in the sixteenth and seventeenth centuries 'so strange and difficult as to be a subject of controversy' (Baugh & Cable). 'Expensive' derives ultimately from the Latin *expendere*, meaning 'to pay in full', which became Medieval Latin *expensa*, meaning 'money for expenses'; from this developed the Old French *espense* and Anglo-Norman and Middle English *expense*. 'Expensive' first appeared around 1630. 'To expend' appears in Cawdrey's dictionary of 1604, but with the meaning 'to consider or muse upon', a meaning that became obsolete in the eighteenth century.

Grocer. Johnson felt that 'grocer' should be spelt 'grosser', though by the mid-eighteenth century a 'grocer' had ceased to be a wholesaler, one who dealt in 'gross' quantities. The spelling *grosser* was in use when the word was adopted from Old French in the fourteenth century; the Worshipful Company of Grocers was founded in 1345 by a group of spice traders, members of the Ancient Guild of Pepperers, to protect their large-scale importing interests. A late seventeenth-century account of the Grocers' Company states that the term was used because 'they sold Gross quantities by great Weights' (*OED*), and in 1582 Mulcaster recommended the spelling 'groce' for 'bulk'. Johnson also gave the possible definition 'or from *grossus*, a fig, which their present state seems to favour'; his *Dictionary* includes occasional personal and topical comments, which may be the case here. If so, its relevance is no longer immediately apparent.

Nest-egg. Before 1325 the word 'nest-egg' was in use for the false egg placed in the nest to encourage hens to lay; the logical expectation from this would be that a financial 'nest-egg' would be primarily a 'non-realisable fund that would encourage usable money to grow round it', rather than an 'amount of money not to be broken into'. However, the *OED* dates the first use of the term in this way to the beginning of the nineteenth century. Previous uses, from the seventeenth century, are a 'reserve of money saved for an emergency', which have prevailed, an example of usage taking a phrase away from its logical meaning – breaking into a china egg would not access much in the way of nutrition.

Pound. Working backwards and by analogy we can work out that there was almost definitely an undocumented Latin word *pondus*, meaning 'weight' (from which we get 'ponderous'). This word was adopted early on by several Germanic languages and was brought to England during the early waves of migration in the fifth and sixth centuries. The Middle English spelling of *pund* gave way to *pound* in the fourteenth century, but the standard plural did not have a final *s* until much later; expressions like 'a ten-pound note' show the retention of this plural without *s*. The financial meaning of the word, deriving from a 'pound of silver', appears in Old English and was probably used implicitly to denote 'money' very early.

Purchase. The early French versions of 'purchase' in use in England after the Conquest are to do with effort and striving. The second half of the word takes us back to the Middle English sense of 'purchase', 'hunting or taking by force'. During the thirteenth century this developed into the sense of 'to acquire possessions or wealth', then 'to acquire property by means other than by inheritance', and then during the fourteenth century 'to acquire something by exchange of money'. Its first use in Middle English dates to around 1300, but its first use in the sense of 'to buy' was in 1390. The sense of 'gaining hold of something' developed into the nautical use of 'purchasing an anchor', i.e. 'hauling it up', so that by the mid-eighteenth century 'purchase' also meant 'grip or leverage'.

Queue. An 'animal's tail' in Latin was *cauda,* which became *coda*. In Middle French and Anglo-Norman this became *queue*, which was eventually adopted into English in the late fifteenth century. The word 'cue' derives from the same source and was the spelling adopted for a plait of hair, documented from 1731, the tail-like billiard cue from 1749, and the actor's cue (dependent on the 'tail' of the previous speech) from the sixteenth century. The first documented use of the word 'queue' for a line of people comes in Carlyle's *French Revolution*: 'That talent ... of spontaneously standing in a queue, distinguishes ... the French People', 1837 (*OED*); though there is an intriguing quote in the *OED* mentioning a 'qwew', possibly a line of dancers, dating from around 1500. It is clear, however, that the custom and the word were borrowed from the French.

Shop. The Middle Low German term *schoppe* corresponding to the Old English *sceoppa*, was 'porch'. This word was used to translate, or maybe just to attempt to pronounce, the Medieval Latin *gazophylacium*,

meaning a 'church strong-box or treasury', in a translation of the Bible. The Anglo-Norman and Old French *eschoppe* was a 'booth, lean-to or stall'. These give the idea of 'a temporary or non-dedicated space', and the idea of a 'shop' as a specific building where goods are sold did not appear till the fifteenth century, when the word was 'shoppe'. The spelling 'shop' developed about 1600.

Stock. The Germanic root *stok* gave rise to the Old English *stocce*, meaning 'tree-stump or log', which developed a number of meanings, including 'hollow receptacle', from the fourteenth century; the 'large back part of a gun', from the sixteenth century; a 'genealogical group of ancestors', from the fourteenth century; in the fifteenth century, the 'upper or lower part of hose', which became 'stockings'; and a 'fund or store of money', in the fifteenth century, which developed into a 'store of goods' by the seventeenth century. This last meaning appeared only in English and developed around 1700 into the financial usage, as in 'stocks and shares'. In July 1773 a group of brokers resolved to rename New Jonathan's, the coffee house where 'stocks' had been traded since 1698, as the Stock Exchange.

Transport

Accident. An 'accident' was originally anything that happened, from the Latin *accidere*, meaning 'to fall or happen', which is retained in the slightly archaic-sounding phrase 'by happy accident'. The Latin *accidens*, meaning 'falling or happening', was adopted almost exactly into Middle English. The sense of 'anything unintended or non-essential' also occurs in the use of the word in the fields of grammar and logic. But there was no logical and historical development from these to the sense of something we would prefer not to happen; since the fourteenth century 'accidents', with adverse effects, have existed side by side with the phrase 'by accident', which retains the sense of a neutral unplanned event.

Bridge. The Old English *brycg* is related to the Old Frisian *brigge* and *bregge* and the Old Saxon *bruggia*. The Old Norse word *bryggja* developed into the word *brig* in northern English dialect, an illustration of a pattern of northern forms retaining a hard consonant that appeared as a softened form in the south (see **egg**). *Bryggja* had the sense of a 'landing-stage or gangway', which may point to a more general Germanic root, which the *Oxford Dictionary of English Etymology* suggests may have been a 'log road'. The word appears as 'brig' in a number of place-names. In Middle English the word appeared as *brugge, bregge, brigge* and *brudge*, and the forms 'bruge' and 'bregge', as well as 'bridge', are found in the sixteenth century. The letter *d* in the middle appeared as a result of the pronunciation, where *-ge* follows a short vowel, as in 'fridge' and 'lodge'.

Bus. Bus is an abbreviation for *omnibus*, the Latin word meaning 'for all'. First recorded in English in 1829, the word had been used in France the previous year and is recorded as being shortened to 'bus' by 1832. However, neither 'bus' nor 'omnibus' appeared in Reid's *Dictionary* in 1853. William Barnes, a Victorian poet and advocate of the use of Old English as a root for new words, proposed that the word 'omnibus' should be replaced by 'folkwain'.

Car. A 'car' is not, as might be expected from the abbreviations of other forms of transport (see **bus**), a shortened form of 'carriage'. The word appeared in the fourteenth century as *carre*, adopted from Norman French *carre*, itself from Late Latin *carra*, 'two-wheeled cart'. *Carra* seems to have been a Celtic root, with varieties of the word occurring in the Celtic languages. From Late Latin the word spread into the German, Dutch, Swedish and Danish languages. The final *-re* dropped off during the seventeenth century, and the word later came to assume a poetic use and a sense of ceremony, as in Lord Nelson's 'funeral car'. The first use of the word for an automobile is in the composite 'motor-car'; 'A name has not yet been found for horseless carriages … The latest suggestion we have had is "motor car"', reported the *Daily Chronicle* in October 1895 (*OED*).

Coach. It seems improbable, but there is general agreement that this word derives from an area of Hungary called Kocs, where coaches were made. In 1556 this word appeared in English, as 'coche', having travelled across Europe and being adopted in variant forms in many European languages. The *OED* says that it is not clear what particular characteristic of the carriage design from Kocs led to its wide adoption; but, language change being an evolutionary process, this may just have been the right sounding word at the right time. The modern spelling was well established by the end of the seventeenth century.

In Barclay's *Dictionary*, in 1812, 'to coach' people meant 'to convey them by coach'. Whether literally or figuratively, this led to the idea of 'coaching' to mean 'taking students or athletes in training along a journey towards higher achievement'.

Commuter. In 1848 railway passengers were able to buy a 'commutation-ticket' for $5, countersigned by B. Fish, which entitled them to make eight journeys between Trenton and New Brunswick, New Jersey, by any line on the route (*OED*). By 1865 'commuters' in the United States could be people who travelled to work by road or rail, but the word was not used in the United Kingdom in this sense until the 1930s. Previously, 'commuting' carried other meanings, including reciprocal exchange, alteration, ransoming, as well as reducing a payment (penal or otherwise), or regulating the direction of an electric current, both of which have been retained. It derives from Latin words meaning 'to change completely'.

Drive. This word has undergone a variety of changes since the Old English *drifan*. While the form of the present tense has remained fairly consistent over the past thousand years, the past tense, now 'drove', and the past participle 'driven' have had a number of forms, including the apparently regular 'drived' and 'drived'. 'Drafe' or 'drave', a northern form for the past tense, was dominant until the late seventeenth century, while *drof, dreof* and *drife* were in use from the thirteenth to the fifteenth centuries. As regards the past participle, 'droven' and 'drove' survived until the eighteenth century; 'drove' was used as a past participle by Nelson in a letter of 1799 (*OED*).

Journey. A 'journey' was once the amount one could travel in a day, though this would vary depending on whether it was done on foot or on horseback; Johnson's *Dictionary* in 1755, Barclay's *Dictionary* in 1812 and Webster's *Dictionary* in 1828 still gave this meaning. The word came into English from the Anglo-Norman *journee*, meaning 'day's work'. The word derives from the Latin *dies*, meaning 'day', and until about 1650 the word was used to mean 'day'. The spelling was established by 1600. Most of the earlier variations involved the use of *i* for the first letter; *i* and *j* became fully distinct from each other only in the mid-nineteenth century.

Kerb. 'Kerb' seems ultimately to derive from 'curved', in the sense of a 'curved or arched piece of stone or metal used structurally', for example at the top of a well, to support the cover. But this usage, dating from the sixteenth century, was modified by association with the word 'curb', meaning 'to restrain or hold', which was part of the function of the structural support, and the sense of curvature was lost during the eighteenth and nineteenth centuries. The development from 'curb', through 'kirb', to 'kerb' took a long time, and through the nineteenth century both 'curb' and 'kerb' were in use for 'the edge of a pavement'.

Roundabout. There is a frequently quoted story that it was an American writer, Logan Pearsall Smith, who in 1927 suggested to the BBC Advisory Committee on Spoken English that the name 'roundabout' should be given to the traffic routing system that had been in use since 1901. However, *Hansard* reports mention 'a roundabout system of traffic' being discussed in July 1927; and the *Glasgow Herald* in January 1927 warned of 'the roundabout' as an inconvenience to pedestrians. It seems likely that this word, in use from the eighteenth century for carousels, round dances and circuitous journeys, was an obvious replacement for the expression 'gyratory circuses' used until then, though 'traffic circle' and 'rotary' are used in other parts of the English-speaking world.

Taxi. This is a 'cab fitted with a taximeter', a device that measures how far the vehicle has travelled. A taximeter meters or measures (from Greek *metron*, 'measure'), 'meter' being a word that came to English from French in the seventeenth century. Inevitably, what is being measured in this case is ultimately a tax, though this may seem a little harsh for a transaction between passenger and cab-driver; in the thirteenth century 'to tax' meant 'to calculate a fine', from the Latin *taxare*, meaning 'to censure or value'.

Traffic. In 1853 'traffic' still meant primarily 'trade or commerce', a sense retained in the phrase 'people trafficking' or 'drug trafficking'. Johnson's *Dictionary* ends many words *-ick* where we now prefer *-ic*, but the *k* has been retained when the word is followed by *-ing*, as in 'trafficking', 'picnicking', 'panicking'. For Johnson 'traffick' was 'commerce' and later 'commodities', and while the sense of commercial movement is still in use it has taken on connotations of illegality or immorality. The use of the word for the movement of vehicles dates from the early nineteenth century, while 'traffic lights' date from as recently as the 1920s.

Tram. A 'tramcar' was the full name from 1873 for a vehicle that travelled along a tramway, originally a system for transporting coal or ore out of a mine. In 1861, the year of the first attempt to introduce trams on to the streets of London, *Chambers Dictionary* still defined 'tramway' only as a 'rude form of railroad for temporary or military purposes, originally for trams (coal wagons) to run on', though trams had been operating in other British cities for over fifty years. 'Tram-road' dates from 1800, and 'tram-way' from 1825 (*OED*). The word comes from the name for a 'beam of a wheelbarrow', first used in the sixteenth century, transferring to the container itself, which eventually became a four-wheeled truck running on rails.

Wheel. The wide range of words in western languages to do with 'turning' suggests an Indo-European root something like *quel-*. In Old English this developed as *hweoghol*, *hweowol* and *hweol*, which survived into Middle English. By the end of the thirteenth century scribes had begun to drop the *h* as a first consonant in a cluster, so that *hr* became *r-* (*hring* to 'ring'), *hl-* became *l-* (*hlaf* to 'loaf'), and *hw* became *w-* or *wh-*. In some dialects, especially in the north, *wh-* was spelt *qu-*, as in the *Cursor Mundi*, written in northern England around 1300; this meant that at the extreme edge of western Europe the spelt form of the word, *quele*, had returned to the spoken form of the conjectural Indo-European root.

Work

Boss. 'Boss' was once thought to be an early migrant word taken from Holland to North America at the time when New York was New Amsterdam (up to 1674), a development from the Dutch *baas*, meaning 'master or employer'. It was recorded as being the name for a 'ship's master' in the seventeenth century and was probably adopted into English during that period of alternate maritime war and peace between Holland and England. There is documentation of the word as 'base', meaning 'foreman', in 1635 in Massachusetts Bay. There is no documentation of the word spelt 'boss' before 1822, and Webster did not record the word used in this sense.

Broker. If some uncertainty attaches to the current meaning of the activities of a 'broker', this reflects views on the word's etymology. Was a 'broker' in fact a 'broacher', one who opened and sold the contents of casks of wine or beer? Or one who inspected goods for 'breakages'? Or someone who, after being declared 'bankrupt', ('broken bench') was allowed to act only as a go-between? Or was the word derived from the Latin *procurator*, 'someone who procures goods or services', or the Old English *bruccan*, meaning 'to be busy'? All of these have their supporters. The *OED* proposes the Old French word *brochier* for the trader who opened casks with a *brocca*, a 'spike', and sold the contents on. However, Wedgwood quotes the fourteenth-century poem *Piers Plowman*, which has a *brocoure*, whose job was to inspect goods for breakages. This word's similarity to Russian and Lithuanian words for 'to break' indicates an origin in the Hanseatic trades.

Whichever we prefer, 'brokers' were well established as middlemen by the beginning of the fifteenth century.

Clerk. Some words were borrowed from Latin twice during the Old English period, one of these being the Latin *clericus*; the first time it appeared as *cliroc*, the second time as *cleric*. There are a number of reasons why this pattern of repeat borrowing happened; one reason often proposed is the low level of communication between centres of learning and influence. But this does not stand up to close examination; while communications during the period were poor, missionaries were energetic travellers, and words relating to administration would have been widely circulated. A stronger possibility is that localised accents and sound changes may have led to a reintroduction of the word as a reaffirmation of the link to Rome.

As scholarship existed almost exclusively within the church during the early medieval period, almost all scholars were either clerics or attached to the church, and the word *clerke*, the version that appeared in the thirteenth century, became applicable to all notaries, copyists, secretaries and accountants. The sixteenth-century spelling 'clark' may have followed the pronunciation. The modern spelling dates from the late sixteenth century.

Engine. The Latin *ingenium*, meaning 'skill or natural ability', became the Old French *engin*, with the senses of 'skill' and 'machine'. Chaucer uses *engin*, with 'memory' and 'intellect', as one of the three 'sapiences'. From this derived the idea of 'something which displayed or was the product of ingenuity' (from the same root), a 'mechanical device'; Robert of Brunne described in about 1330 how giants used 'engines' to set the stones of Stonehenge. As technology advanced, the word came to be applied to more or less any mechanism, from a microscope in 1662, to a pair of scissors by Pope in *The Rape of the Lock* (1714), to manufacturing equipment by Adam Smith in *The Wealth of Nations* in 1776. There also developed the Middle English word *gin*, a contrivance, which in the thirteenth century developed connotations of 'spring' and 'trap'.

Factory. A 'factory' was originally a 'trading house', where goods were exchanged and sometimes stored; the term was used for an establishment in a foreign country, usually associated with Portuguese merchants and the East India Company in India and south-east Asia, and then China. The word continued to be used in this way until the mid-nineteenth century, though by the 1830s it was used for a 'place of manufacture' (literally 'making by hand'). The root word is the Latin *factum*, meaning 'having been made', from the verb *facere*, meaning 'to make or do'. Partridge points out that the Late Latin word *factorium*, meaning an 'oil-mill or oil-press', suggested the form of the word 'factory', and the first documentation of the word is also for a 'press', in 1618, but in this case a printing press, set up by the Stationers' Company in London.

Office. The Latin root word *officium* is derived from two words, *opus* and *ficere*, a form of *facere*, together meaning 'to do work'. This developed into the Old French *office* and the Middle English 'office', which was adopted for a wide range of usages, dividing into three groups, to do with a workplace, religious ceremony, and a formal duty. The idea of an 'office' as a workplace can be dated back to the late fourteenth century, and the late stage of this development of the meaning of the word can be seen in its position in the chronologically ordered listings of definitions in various dictionaries. In Johnson's *Dictionary* in 1790 it is eighth, after usages to do with duties and devotions, eleventh in the *Chambers Twentieth Century Dictionary* (1972) and sixth in the *Concise Oxford Dictionary* (1974), behind such entries as a 'piece of kindness, attention, service'.

Salary. The story that Roman soldiers were paid in salt, and that this is the derivation of 'salary', used to be one of the most widely known English etymologies; and it is nearly correct. Webster's doubt about the story is shown at the beginning of the entry: 'Said to be from …' The Latin *salarium* was originally a 'payment to soldiers for the purchase of salt' and came into Middle English by way of Anglo-Norman *salarie*. It is first documented in 1377 and was applied to chantry priests (those paid to sing masses regularly for the salvation of someone who had left money for that purpose). Roman legionaries between about 100 BC and AD 100 were paid 225 *denarii* per annum.

Tycoon. 'Tycoon' was an honorific name applied in nineteenth-century Japan to the Shogun, the hereditary commander-in-chief and ruler, until the post was abolished in 1868. When first used by Europeans it was spelt 'taikun'. The Japanese word derives from the Chinese for 'great prince'. The first person in the West to be called a 'tycoon' was Abraham Lincoln, and the use of the word to describe a successful businessman appeared in the 1920s.

Abstract Nouns

Aftermath. We think now of the 'aftermath' of an event being an undesired consequence, but this word has changed its meaning in the past two hundred years. The 'aftermath' used to be the second crop of grass in a meadow after the first crop was cut for hay, and it was thus something desirable. The *math* part comes from the Old English word for 'to mow' and is related to the word 'meadow' (literally a place where grass is grown for cutting); in Webster's *Dictionary* 'math' means a 'mowing'. 'Aftermath' was still used in this way in the mid-nineteenth century, when it began to be used more figuratively. Its sense of being 'events or the situation following something being destroyed', as in the 'aftermath of the storm', developed from its earlier application.

Alarm. Johnson pointed out the derivation of 'alarm' from the French *à l'arme*, meaning 'to arms', but it had come to French from the Italian *all'arme*. Initially a call of warning, the word became first the name of such a call, and then the verb meaning 'to call someone to arms'. Contemporary stage directions for Shakespeare's plays include the phrase 'alarums and excursions', meaning people arming themselves and fighting; the development of 'alarum' as an alternative form happened in the fourteenth century and lasted till the seventeenth, supposedly deriving from a rolled *r* to prolong the second half of the word. This produced other spellings such as 'larum' and 'larem', now lost, as well as 'al-arm', recommended by Mulcaster in 1582. It was not until the mid-seventeenth century that 'to alarm' developed into the meaning of 'to upset or cause disturbance'.

Comfort. 'Comfort' used to be a much stronger idea than a kind word, a soft cushion or a shoulder to cry on, and the words 'force', 'fortify' and 'fortress' show a closer connection to the root word, the Latin *fors*, meaning 'strength'. Brown proposes that 'comforts for the troops would once have been allies and reinforcements', but this sense fell out of use in the eighteenth century; for Cockeram, already in 1623, the meaning was 'consolation'. The current sense of the verb as 'to soothe physically or mentally' has been in use since the fourteenth century, while the sense of 'to strengthen' was becoming obsolete by the time Webster included it in his 1828 *Dictionary*. The abstract sense of the noun as 'wellbeing' has been in use since the word was first adopted from Old French in the fourteenth century.

Danger. In the late twelfth century *daunger* meant 'arrogance, the power of a master', perhaps reflecting the relationship still existing between Saxon and Norman. Someone 'dangerous' was 'difficult to please or to deal with'; 'danger' thus came to mean 'liability to punishment, hesitation, reluctance' and, by the fourteenth century, 'liability to injury'. The idea of 'danger' as the 'power to cause injury' continued into the eighteenth century. The word came into English from the Middle French *dangier* or *dongier*, meaning a 'lord's power or jurisdiction'. The Latin root is the word for 'lordship', *dominium*, and the *ni* sound may indicate a link to the Spanish *hacer daño*, meaning 'to hurt'.

Delight. 'Delight' has no etymological connection with 'light', but comes from the Old and Middle French *deleitier*, and ultimately the Latin *delectare*, meaning 'to draw out from or seduce' and thus figuratively 'to delight'. The early spellings *delit* and *delyte* were in use from the thirteenth century to the late sixteenth, but by the early sixteenth century spellings ending with *-ght* had begun to take over, probably as a result of a connection between sound and sense. The spelling 'light' was a result of the direct continuation from the Old English *leoht* and the Middle English *liht* to the early Modern English *lyght*, in which the consonant sound before the *t* would have been clearly audible.

Enthusiasm. 'Enthusiasm' is constructed from Greek words *en* and *theos*, meaning 'in' and 'god', literally 'possessed by a god'. In the seventeenth century it was used to mean 'fury inspired by a god', and only in the eighteenth century did it develop the sense of 'eager interest'. In between, the spirit of reason defined 'enthusiasmos' as 'a vain belief of private revelation; a vain confidence of divine favour or communication' (Johnson), rising, according to Locke, 'from the conceits of a warmed or overweening imagination'.

Fruition. Whether or not one takes the position that judgements of right or wrong are largely irrelevant to language change, 'fruition' is noticeably a word in provocative transition; but it has been a rather long transition. What might look like a sixteenth-century inkhorn term was in fact in use much earlier, the *OED* documenting it from 1416. It comes from the Latin verb *frui*, meaning 'to enjoy', and originally had nothing to do with fruit or bearing fruit. Even the *OED* describes this as an erroneous association, showing its colours with the words: 'the blunder was not countenanced by nineteenth-century Dictionaries in this country, nor by Webster or Worcester, though it was somewhat common both in England and in the US.' The *OED* records the sense of 'coming into fruit or fulfilment' as appearing in the *Century Dictionary* in 1889, and the first recorded use of the phrase 'bring to fruition' in 1958. 'Fruition' in accordance with its Latin root means the 'action of enjoyment; pleasurable possession' (*OED*), but in the preface to a 2008 book on etymology it was used in the sense of completion.

Fuss. Condemned by Johnson as a 'low' word, 'fuss' has puzzled etymologists. Wedgwood dismissed Skeat's idea that it came from Old English *fus* meaning 'prompt or quick', preferring the idea that it copied the sound of air coming out of a bottle, 'puffing and blowing' as the *OED* puts it. Partridge agreed that the word echoed a sound but noted the similarity to German *fusseln*, meaning 'to walk unsteadily', though this is a rather tenuous link. The word appeared in the early eighteenth century and may perhaps be a happy invention of popular speech.

Mystery. Cawdrey in 1604 defined a mystery as 'a secret, or hid thing'. In the sense of 'something deliberately kept close', it came to mean by the fourteenth century the 'protected skills of an occupation'. The word was later used for a 'religious truth or doctrine', and in the eighteenth century for a 'medieval play explaining such ideas'. It comes from a conjectured Anglo-Norman word *misterie*, or possibly directly from the Latin *mysterium,* in turn deriving from the Greek *musterion,* 'secret thing or ceremony'. There is a link to words such as 'mystical' or 'mysticism', all deriving from the Greek *mustes*, 'initiated person', an idea which can be seen in the eighteenth-century use of 'mysteries' for the 'hidden knowledge of a secret society'.

Noise. 'A group of sounds heard together' has been a meaning of this word since the thirteenth century, when the word was adopted from Anglo-Norman. This derived from the Old French *noise* or *noyse*, meaning 'noise or tumult', which developed into various ideas 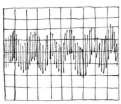 surrounding unrest; these had ultimately come from the Latin *nausea*, meaning 'disgust or annoyance'. Various English dialects maintained the sense of 'unrest' or 'quarrel' up to the early twentieth century. For a period in the sixteenth century your 'noise' was your 'reputation', a usage which has been retained in the phrase 'a big noise in the world of ...' See **annoy** and **nuisance**.

Nuisance. If 'nuisance' is a word that we know but would find it hard to define, this perhaps comes from the way it has developed over time. Johnson noted that it came from the French word of the same spelling and meant 'something noxious or offensive, or in law, something that incommodes the neighbourhood'. *Chambers Dictionary* in 1882 noted the link to the word 'annoy' but also noted that the Latin *noxa*, meaning 'something that hurts', and *nausea*, meaning 'disgust or annoyance', led to the word 'noise', and the now lost word 'noisome'. While the legal meaning has lasted from the fifteenth century to the present and might range from 'polluting a water supply' to 'building over a neighbour's land', in common speech since the early nineteenth century the tone of the word has calmed to something mildly vexing but not harmful. See **annoy** and **noise**.

Panic. 'Panic' comes originally from the Greek phrase *to panikon deima*, meaning 'fear of the god Pan', which was shortened to *panikon*. This was adopted into French in the sixteenth century as *panique* and entered English as *panicque*, more as an adjective, 'panic terror', than as a noun, and originally with the meaning 'to do with the god Pan'. It was not until the mid-seventeenth century that 'panic' was used in the sense of 'sudden uncontrollable fear', though the ninth edition of Johnson's *Dictionary* in 1790 still listed 'panick' only as an adjective, meaning 'violent without cause.'

Patriotism. 'Patriotism' shows how a word is built up from Greek via other languages. 'Patriot' comes from the Latin *patria*, meaning 'one's native land' ('motherland' or 'fatherland'),  deriving from *pater*, meaning 'father', adopted by Latin from Greek. The *-ot* suffix comes from the Greek *-otes*, meaning 'inhabitant of', usually via Latin *-ota*; and the *-ism* comes from the Greek *-ismos*, via Latin *-ismus* and/or French *-isme*, and means 'the state of being' the word it is joined to. While Johnson may have claimed in conversation that patriotism was 'the last refuge of a scoundrel', he defined it in his *Dictionary* as 'love of one's country; zeal for one's country'.

Sorrow. 'Sorrow', which in Old English was *sorg* and *sorh*, and in Middle English became *sorge*, *sorwe* and later *sorewe*, belongs to a group of words expressing 'care' or 'anxiety' common to most Germanic languages. For example, Dutch has *zorg*, Gothic had *saúrga*, and Old Norse had *sorg*. Despite appearances, 'sorry' is unrelated; it derives from Old English *sarig*, meaning 'distressing or painful', which became Middle English *sari*, and in northern and Scottish dialects the form with *a* was retained until the nineteenth century. The change of the vowel in the south to the current sound that makes it look like an adjective derived from 'sorrow' is misleading.

Adjectives

Antique. The Latin *antiquus*, meaning 'ancient', gave rise to two meanings in English, both spelt 'antik' or 'antick': 'grotesque' and 'ancient'. The second of these meanings developed the additional spelling 'antique' in the early part of the sixteenth century, obviously under French influence. Henry VIII appointed John Leland as England's only official 'Antiquary' in 1533 to research the 'antiquities' of England. The spelling 'antique' became established over the course of the seventeenth century; Johnson noted the change of pronunciation happening during his lifetime, as the stress moved from the first to the second syllable. After the word 'grotesque' became established, from the mid-sixteenth century, 'antic' seemed to fall away into the sense of 'ridiculous behaviour', though the sense of 'strange' still lingered around the word. Johnson's *Dictionary* in 1822 carried the definition 'odd' under the entry for 'antique'.

Blank. 'Blank', meaning 'empty', is derived from the Old French word for 'white', arriving in Middle English as *blank, blonc* and *blaunc*. It is a word we may easily link to similar words in the Romance languages Spanish, French, Italian and Portuguese, but, as David Crystal points out, we look in vain for a Latin root, since the Latin for 'white' is *albus* (the name 'Albion' for Britain comes from the white cliffs of Dover, the first aspect of the country seen by the Romans). In Germanic languages other than English we find words similar to 'blank' meaning either 'bright', 'shining' or 'horse' (Old English *blanca*, 'horse'). Bearing in mind that a white horse has in many cultures been seen as something more than just a horse that happens to be white, this suggests that the Germanic word was adopted in the western parts of the Roman world, but with the symbolic meanings that were projected on to a white horse.

Crisp. Cawdrey defined 'crisped' as 'curled or frisled', the verb originally meaning 'to make the pattern of tightly curled hair, or to ruffle the surface of water, or to construct the pattern of a ruff'. The earliest applications of 'crisp' as an adjective, from the tenth century, are to do with making hair wavy. It is tempting to imagine a development of the meaning by thinking that the same processes that make something curly also make it brittle – an early fifteenth-century text describes how putting paper in an oven makes it 'blak and crisp', while a variant text describes it as 'blakk and runklid' (*OED*); but this ignores the many instances of the word describing the surface of disturbed water. The sense of 'brittleness' appeared in the fifteenth century and developed towards 'hardness' in the nineteenth and twentieth centuries. Appropriately crisps are seldom flat.

Defunct. The Latin verb *defungi* meant 'to complete something or finish with it', thus *defunctus* meant 'finished with, i.e. dead'. Ben Jonson was one of the strongest critics of 'defunct' when it was apparently a new word at the beginning of the seventeenth century, but its first recorded use in English is at the end of the fourteenth century (*OED*). The spelling has been remarkably consistent since Shakespeare's use of it in *Henry V*, in which he also coined the word 'defunction' meaning 'death'. The connection with 'function' is clear, but it is interesting that usage has retained 'defunct' and 'malfunction', but not 'defunction' or 'malfunct'.

Dismal. In the medieval church calendar twenty-four days were regarded as bad, two per month; these had been computed by Egyptian astrologers and were accepted into Roman culture as bad days for initiating an enterprise. The Latin for 'bad day', *dies malus*, became Old French *dis mal*, and thus Middle English *dismale*, used originally as a noun. By the late sixteenth century it had become an adjective, often referring to days, as it were referring to itself – thus Mulcaster in 1582 has the word 'dismaldaie', effectively meaning 'day bad day'. During the seventeenth century 'dismal' came to be used to describe weather, environments and eventually anything miserable or gloomy.

Equal. 'It is most equal that men should choose their religion themselves,' wrote Thomas Helwes in 1612, using 'equal' in the sense of 'fair and just'; this was the meaning of the Latin *æquus*, which developed into the Old French *equal*, a sense now conveyed by the word 'equitable'. There was a now obsolete word used in Middle and early Modern English which was spelt *egall*, from the Old French *egal*, from the Latin *æqualis*, meaning 'equal'. The English 'equal' developed its meaning of 'the same or of the same level' during the sixteenth century, while the sense of 'fair' died out during the eighteenth century.

Extravagant. The Latin *vagus*, meaning 'wandering', has given English a number of words including 'vague' and 'vagabond'. Arriving via Medieval Latin, *extravagant* was first used in English in 1387, in the sense of something 'wandering outside its proper bounds', to describe a papal decree that was not collected into the set which would confirm it as part of canon law. Shakespeare used the word to describe the ghost of Hamlet's father, in 1602. It was not until the beginning of the eighteenth century that the word was used in the sense of 'wild and generous spending or giving'.

Faithful. Old English's ability to create words from words can be seen in the application of the suffix *-ful* or *-full* to create an adjective from a noun, as in *wuldorfull*, meaning 'glorious', from *wuldor*, meaning 'glory'. The Latin *fides*, meaning 'faith', developed into the Old French *feid* or *feit*, which became *fei*, and then the Middle English *feit*, *feith* or *fayth*, to which was added the Old English suffix *-full*. *Faithful* appeared as early as 1300, and the spelling with one *l* was fairly well established in the sixteenth century, though the second *l*, applied in Mulcaster's *Elementarie* in 1582, did not entirely disappear until the eighteenth century.

Fast. If the two meanings of 'fast', 'quick' and 'secure', appear to contradict, an explanation may be found in Johnson's proposed alternative derivations, one from the Old Welsh *ffest*, meaning 'quick', and the other from the Old English *fast*, meaning 'fixed'. It is more likely that the sense of 'quick' developed from the meaning 'secure', in the sense of 'firm', and 'maintaining a hold'. Webster explained this: 'the sense of "swift" comes from the idea of keeping close to what is pursued.' The root idea in a range of Germanic languages is 'firm', which in the sense of 'keeping hold of an objective' connects to 'fast', as in 'to abstain from food', 'fast asleep', 'steadfast', 'a fast dye', and 'to run fast'. Though there are earlier incidences of use, the idea of 'fast' as 'quick' seems to have taken hold in the sixteenth century.

Gay. The earliest recorded use of 'gay' in English is in the early fourteenth century, the word having been adopted from the Old French *gai*, itself probably from a Frankish root meaning 'sudden or impetuous'. Cawdrey in 1604, spelling it as 'gaie', defined it as 'fine, trim'. The meaning of 'gay' as 'homosexual' has more or less suppressed its previous meaning of 'light-hearted or jolly', though there has been a slang sexual connotation to the word since the eighteenth century. Though Wilton proposes that the use of 'gay' for 'homosexual' is a derivation from 'gaycat', in use by 1893 for a 'young male tramp', its use in this sense in American English can be more certainly traced to the 1930s, specifically within the homosexual community. Its wider adoption came in the early 1970s; in the 1972 edition of the *Chambers Twentieth Century Dictionary* it is given as an example of an 'older word having recently acquired a new and highly specialised meaning'.

During the late 1990s the word began to be used in North America as a synonym for 'uncool, unaccepted', among young people, a usage which transferred to Britain around 2002–4 and became common street and school usage. This was eventually picked up and deplored by politicians, since it appeared to be condemning homosexuality, definitely against the ethos being promoted in schools. However, according to Nancy Updike, writing in 2000, the word was being used playfully in this way in the United States among non-homophobic people no longer threatened by its use, and deliberately referring to its condemnatory use in their own childhoods. Among British teenagers these two meanings of the word 'gay' are becoming disassociated, as much as the various meanings of the word 'trunk'.

Naughty. In the fifteenth and sixteenth centuries 'naughty' meant 'vile or wicked', during which time it was also spelt 'nawghty' and 'naughtie'. By the time Webster defined it (and as part of his spelling reform campaign he spelled it 'nauty', though under the entry for 'naughtiness'), the meanings ranged from 'wicked' to 'mischievous', especially as applied to children. Sexual connotations have been around the word since the seventeenth century, but the degree of moral condemnation in the word as applied to adult behaviour has diminished gradually to the point where it is hardly a condemnation at all. The phrase 'naughty but nice' first appeared in a song in 1871.

Nervous. For Samuel Johnson 'nervous' meant first 'well-strung, strong, or vigorous'. Only later did it have a connection to actual nerves, and only after that, in medical jargon, a sense of a person 'having weak nerves'. The idea of the nerves being too sensitive and this leading to anxiety began to appear around the middle of the eighteenth century and has now become the predominant meaning, with a sense of loss of strength. Effectively the word has reversed its meaning, for the Latin *nervus* meant 'sinew or tendon', something which manifested action and strength. 'Nerve' is documented in English from the late fourteenth century, and 'nervous', 'pertaining to or having nerves', from the same time.

New-fangled. We might not expect such a word to have a long pedigree but it appears in Chaucer as early as 1375, as a noun, *newfanglenesse*, meaning 'novelty'. The root gave rise to forms now lost, such as 'newfanglist', in the early seventeenth century, 'a person with a taste for novelty'; 'to newfangle', from the sixteenth to nineteenth centuries, meaning 'to make something new or different'; and, in the sixteenth century, 'newfangly', meaning 'in a newfangled way', and even a re-invention, a 'fangle', meaning 'foppish fashion'. *Fangen* was a Middle English word for 'to seize or grasp', which gave rise to *fangel*, 'silly invention', and thus *newfangel*, 'novelty'. 'Newfangledness or newfangleness' appears in Barclay's *Dictionary* in 1812 as 'vain or foolish love of novelty'.

Outrageous. The Old French *oultrage* and Italian *oltragio* derive from the Latin *ultra* and thus mean 'something going beyond limits'. From the fourteenth century, when the word entered Middle

English, there was an almost unlimited series of spellings for what is now spelled 'outrageous', including *oultragious, outerragious, owtreages, owtragews, outradious* and *uttragius*. Cawdrey defined 'outrageous' as 'fierce, unreasonable', and Defoe used it in the late seventeenth century for a river bursting its banks. But over the centuries the meanings of physical violence, still there in the slightly archaic phrase 'to commit an outrage', have calmed to give more of a feeling of 'shocking and socially unacceptable'.

Ready. Johnson believed this word may have been linked to the Old English *hrathe* meaning 'nimble', but Old English had *ræde*, meaning 'equipped' or 'ready', which became Middle English *redi* and then *readi*. All the Germanic languages have similar forms, from Old Norse *reidr* ('ready') to Gothic *garaiths* ('established'); Gothic was

spoken between the fourth and the ninth century mostly in the southern parts of central and eastern Europe, but also in Spain and Portugal. The *Oxford Dictionary of English Etymology* and Eric Partridge both suggest a connection between 'ready' and 'ride', in the sense of being prepared for a journey. Webster proposed that 'ready, ride, read, riddle, are all of one family, and probably from the root of Latin *gradi*, meaning "to advance".'

Strange. The Middle French word *estrange* meaning 'external or foreign' came from the Latin *extraneus*, which is derived from the Latin root *extra*, meaning 'on the outside', from *ex*, 'out of'. The word entered Middle English in the thirteenth century as *strange* or *straunge*. In seventeenth-century England, when the parish was the basic administrative unit, anyone unknown and from outside the parish was a 'stranger'; thus the burial of 'a strange boie' is documented in the church records for East Greenwich in May 1622. The idea of 'unusual' has existed in the use of the word from the fourteenth century, while the sense of 'apart' still exists in the word 'estranged'.

Wrong. In Old English *wr* at the beginning of a word was pronounced as two separate consonant sounds, a pronunciation that survived in some parts of the country till the beginning of the eighteenth century. 'Wrong' appeared in Old English as *wrange*, as the Old Norse word *wrangr* replaced the Old English *unriht* ('not right'). 'Unright' survived as an adjective and noun into the sixteenth century but became rare after that, though it does appear in Johnson's 1755 *Dictionary*. 'Wrong' was used first as a noun and only later as an adjective.

Verbs

Accommodate. In one of the more notorious spellings in English, the double consonants come from the butting up of prefixes, which would be separated as *ad+com+modus*. The root *commodus* means 'convenient or advantageous'; thus the extension by the addition of *ad*, often adapted to *ac* in compound words, meaning 'to', gives the sense of 'giving help or shelter to'. In 1878 George Harley campaigned vigorously for the abolition of doubled letters, claiming that 'the coresponding part of the British public, through the instrumentality of leters alone, anualy send through the post-ofice over twenty thousand milions of unecesary leters of the alphabet'.

Annoy. In 1604 Cawdrey defined 'noysome' as 'hurtful', deriving not from an earlier form of 'noise', but from the application of the suffix *-some*, meaning 'having or bearing' (as in 'cumbersome'), to the word 'noy', from the Anglo-Norman *nui* or *nuye*, meaning 'to annoy'. 'Noisome' served the need for a word with meanings ranging from 'disagreeable' to 'injurious' until the twentieth century, when it began to disappear. By Johnson's time 'to noie', meaning 'to annoy', was 'an old word disused', and Bailey noted that 'to noie' and 'noiance' had become 'to annoy' and 'annoyance'. The level of stress occasioned by 'annoying' someone has gradually lessened over time from the fourteenth century, though until the nineteenth century there was a military application which included bombarding an enemy town. See **noise** and **nuisance**.

Ascertain. For seventeenth- and eighteenth-century writers, especially those trying to redirect the English language away from what they

— 120 —

felt to be chaos and degradation, 'to ascertain' meant 'to make certain and fixed', rather than 'to find out'. For Skinner in 1671 it came from the Latin words *ad* and *certum* and meant 'to affirm', and could be best exemplified by Jonathan Swift's 1712 *Proposal for Correcting, Improving and Ascertaining the English Tongue*. The sense of 'finding out' derives from the sense, documented from the early seventeenth century, of 'making yourself certain about something'. The word came into Middle English from French as *acertein*, which developed into forms such as *asarrtayne*, until spelling revisionists brought back the *c* in the sixteenth century.

Connect. 'Connect' is a relatively late form, in general use only from the seventeenth century. The earlier form, which appears for example in Bullokar's 1616 dictionary, was 'connex', meaning 'to knit or tye together'. This form derived directly from the French *connexer* but is itself recorded only from the mid-sixteenth century (*OED*). In Old English the word *gadrian* was used ('gather' and 'together' derive from this), which became Middle English *gaderen*, but this word died out in the thirteenth century. It seems that the word 'join', adopted from Old French in the thirteenth century, took over.

Consider. The Latin *considerare* became the French *considérer*, which came into Middle English as *considere*, which, with some variants, developed into 'consider' by the sixteenth century. The original meaning may have been 'to contemplate the heavens', since the proposed root word, *sidus*, is Latin for 'star'. But Webster felt the literal sense was 'to sit by or close to something' and thus to 'set the mind or eye' to it.

Cope. In the early nineteenth century 'to cope with' meant 'to fight with or contend with'. The meanings for 'to cope' on its own were given as 'to set an arch over something or to cover', and 'to reward or give in return'. These different ideas all come from different roots whose spellings have converged in the word 'cope'. The sense of fighting comes from the French *couper*, now meaning 'to cut', but formerly meaning 'to hit' (as in the expression *coup d'etat*); 'coping with' a problem means 'contending with' it and has assumed the sense of 'overcoming by contending'. 'To arch or cover' derives from the same root as 'cape' and can be seen in the word 'coping', meaning a 'covering stone'. The now obsolete meaning of 'to reward or pay' comes from the same root as 'cheap' and originally meant 'to buy', but this was obsolete by the seventeenth century, except that perhaps a shadow of it remains in the slang phrase 'to cop it'. The sense of 'successfully contending with difficulties', which has edged out most other uses, can be traced back to the mid-seventeenth century.

Despise. Isidore of Seville proposed that the Latin word *despiciens*, literally meaning 'looking down', was the key to the word 'despise'. Partridge traced this through Old and Middle French to the Middle English *despisen*. It appeared in English in the thirteenth century, occasionally being spelt 'despice', a spelling showing clearly its development from the Latin *despicere*.

Discomfit. The curious word 'discomfiting', not often used, has nothing etymologically to do with 'discomforting' (see **comfort**), though semantically they are similar. 'Discomfit', meaning 'to overcome or thwart' something or someone, comes from the Latin roots *dis* and *conficere*, meaning 'to undo'. During the period of Old French the *n* in *desconfit* became the *m* in *descumfit*; this became the Middle English word *descomfit*, which became 'discomfit' by the fifteenth century. 'Comfit', the positive development from *conficere*, also involved a change from *n* to *m* (but there was a more common parallel development, 'confection'); 'comfit' has to do with sweets and preserves and is not connected to 'comfort' etymologically, though in other ways very much so.

Discover. For Webster the modern sense of 'discover', as 'to find something out for the first time', was the latest definition in a list that included variations of revealing, having the first sight of, and making known; the basic meaning is 'to uncover'. The sense of obtaining new knowledge has been extant since the mid-sixteenth century, and the current spelling is the same as is documented from the fourteenth century, though interim spellings have included *deschuver*, *descure* and *discuir*.

Nibble. 'Nibble' was 'gnible' in Mulcaster's *Elementarie* in 1582. By the time it appeared in the 1824 edition of Johnson's *Dictionary* it was 'nibble', deriving, it was claimed, from the word *nib*, meaning 'beak', 'mouth' or even 'nose' in Old English, which is linked to 'to nip' (and according to Partridge 'nipple'). *Gn-* and *kn-* at the beginning of a word were both pronounced until the sixteenth century.

Rinse. 'Rinse' derives from the Old French *reincier*, probably from a Vulgar Latin conjectural word *recentiare*, meaning 'to make fresh', though the *OED* states the word is 'of uncertain origin'. Partridge linked it to the Latin *recens* meaning 'fresh', itself linked to the word 'recent', while the *OED* points out the similarity to the Old Norse *hreinsa*, meaning 'to cleanse', but states that the similarity is probably accidental. While 'rinsing' now carries the sense of 'washing' but with less thoroughness, formerly 'rinsing' meant 'making clean', even ritually. In the fourteenth and fifteenth centuries, when a priest washed his fingers after communion, this was described as 'rynsande'. Johnson's proposed derivation from the German *rein*, meaning 'clean', deserves some consideration.

Rummage. 'To rummage' in the sixteenth century meant 'to clean out and replace the gravel ballast of a ship', something that had to be done regularly to prevent the hull rotting from the inside. Previously it had meant 'to stow goods in the hold of a ship', and it was not until the eighteenth century that it meant 'to fetch stuff out of the hold'. The word derives originally from Old French *arrumage*, similar to the modern French *arrimage* meaning 'stowage'.

Whinge. 'To whinge' is a surprisingly old word, appearing as *hwinsunge* in the mid-twelfth century to describe 'the whining noise made by dogs'. This developed from the Old English *hwinan*, meaning 'to make the noise of an arrow flying', itself coming from the Old Norse *hvina*. A variety of interesting spellings was used in the following centuries, including *quhyngeand* and *quhingeing*. Partridge links to these the word 'whinny' but relates this also to *hinnire*, the Latin word for 'to neigh'. It is possible that these are all at least partially copying the sounds of a horse or an arrow, and that they overlap. 'Whinge', which became the settled spelling in the seventeenth century, developed into 'winge' in the twentieth century, particularly in the phrase 'wingeing poms'.

Bibliography

Further reading

Almond, J. *Dictionary of Word Origins*. Citadel, 1996.

Barnhart, R. *Chambers Dictionary of Etymology*. Chambers Harrap, 1999.

Baugh, A. C., and Cable, T. *A History of the English Language*. Routledge & Kegan Paul, 2002.

Bragg, M. *The Adventure of English*. Arcade, 2004.

Brown, I. *Chosen Words*. Penguin, 1964.

Bryson, B. *Mother Tongue*. Penguin, 1991.

Cambridge History of the English Language. Cambridge University Press, 2001.

Crystal, D. *Words, Words, Words*. Oxford University Press, 2000.

Crystal, D. *The Cambridge Encyclopaedia of the English Language*. Cambridge University Press, 2002.

Crystal, D. The Stories of English. Allen Lane, 2004.

Crystal, D. *The Fight For English*. Oxford University Press, 2006.

Flavell, L. *Dictionary of Word Origins*. Kyle Cathie, 2004.

Fowler, H. W., and Fowler, F. G. *The Concise Oxford Dictionary of Current English*. Clarendon Press, 1974.

Funk, W. *Word Origins: A Classic Exploration of Words and Language*. Gramercy, USA, 1992.

Green, J. *Cassell's Dictionary of Slang*. Cassell, 2000.

Hilliam, D. *Do You Know English Word Origins?* PRB, Bournemouth, 1996.

Hitchings, H. *Defining the Word: The Extraordinary Story of Dr Johnson's Dictionary*. John Murray, 2005.

Hitchings, H. *The Secret Life of Words: How English Became English*. John Murray, 2008.

Liberman, A. *Word Origins and How We Know Them*. Oxford University Press, USA, 2005.

Liberman, A. *An Analytic Dictionary of English Etymology*. University of Minnesota Press, 2008.

Micklethwait, D. *Noah Webster and the American Dictionary*. McFarland Jefferson, 2000.

Onions, C. T. *The Oxford Dictionary of English Etymology*. Clarendon Press, 1966.

Ostler, N. *Empires of the Word*. Harper Collins, 2005.

Oxford English Dictionary: Compact Edition. Oxford University Press, 1979.

Partridge, E. *Origins*. Routledge & Kegan Paul, 1982.

Pavord, A. *The Naming of Names*. Bloomsbury, 2005.

Roberts, J. *A Thesaurus of Old English*. King's College, London, 1995.

Room, A. *Dictionary of True Etymologies*. Routledge & Kegan Paul, 1986.

Scholl, A. *Bloomers, Biros and Wellington Boots*. O'Mara, 1996.

Scragg, D. *History of English Spelling*. Manchester University Press, 1975.

Sheard, J. A. *The Words We Use*. Andre Deutsch, 1970.

Skeat, W. *A Concise Etymological Dictionary of the English Language*. Clarendon Press, 1882, 1978.

Tulloch, A. *Word Routes*. Peter Owen, 2005.

Weekley, E. *An Etymological Dictionary of Modern English*. Dover, 1968.

Wilton, D. *Word Myths: Debunking Linguistic Urban Legends*. Oxford University Press, New York, 2004.

Yule, H., and Burnell, A. C. *Hobson-Jobson, the Anglo-Indian Dictionary*. Wordsworth, 1996.

Older works referenced

Bailey, N. *An Universal Etymological English Dictionary*. London, 1721.

Barclay, Rev. J. *Complete and Universal Dictionary of the English Language*. Brightly & Childs, Bungay, 1812.

Bullokar, J. *The English Expositor*. London, 1616.

Cawdrey, Robert. *A Table Alphabeticall conteyning and teaching the true writing and vnderstanding of Hard Vsuall Words*. London, 1604. Facsimile published by Edmund Weaver, London, 1966.

Cockeram, H. *The English Dictionarie*. 1623. Later editions enlarged by H. C. Gent.

Cooley, A. *A Dictionary of the English Language*. Chambers, London and Edinburgh, 1861.

Corpus Glossary. About AD 725. Edition published by Cambridge University Press, 1921.

Findlater, A. *Chambers's Etymological Dictionary of the English Language*. Chambers, London and Edinburgh, 1882.

Fowler, F. G. *The King's English*. Clarendon Press, Oxford, 1906.

Isidore of Seville (died AD 636). *The Etymologies*. Translated by P. Throop. Charlotte, Vermont, 2005.

Jespersen, O. *Growth and Structure of the English Language*. Teubner, Leipzig, 1912.

Johnson, A. T., and Smith, H. A. *Plant Names Simplified*. Collingridge, New York, 1958.

Johnson, Samuel. *A Dictionary of the English Language, in which the words are deduced from their originals, and illustrated in their different significations by examples from the best writers*. London, 1755, 1790, 1822.

Lemon, G. W. *English Etymology*. London, 1783.

Macdonald, A. M. (editor). *Chambers Twentieth Century Dictionary*. Chambers, Edinburgh and London, 1972.

Mulcaster, R. *The Elementarie*. 1582. Edition published by Oxford University Press, 1925.

Palmer, A. S. *Folk-etymology, a Dictionary of Verbal Corruptions*. Bell, 1882.

Partridge, E. *From Sanskrit to Brazil, Vignettes and Essays upon Languages*. Hamish Hamilton, London, 1952.

Priestley, J. *Lectures on the Theory of Language and Universal Grammar*. 1762.

Reid, A. *Dictionary of the English Language*. Oliver & Boyd, Edinburgh, 1853.

Serjeantson, M. *A History of Foreign Words in English*. Routledge & Kegan Paul, London, 1935.

Skinner, S. *Etymologicon Linguae Anglicanae*. London, 1671.

Swift, J. *A Proposal for Correcting, Improving and Ascertaining the English Tongue*. London, 1712.

Webster, N. *A Compendious Dictionary of the English Language*. New York, 1806.

Webster, N. *An American Dictionary of the English Language*. New York. First edition, 1828; tenth edition, 1832.

Wedgwood, H. *A Dictionary of English Etymology*. Trubner, London, 1859.

Wedgwood, H. *Contested Etymologies in the Dictionary of the Rev. W. W. Skeat*. Trubner, London, 1882.

Worcester, J. E. *A Dictionary of the English Language*. Boston, 1860.

Index

INDEX